END OF DAYS: 1971 - 2001

UFO over New Mexico, October, 1957.
"And then they will see the Son of Man
coming in a cloud with power and great
glory." Luke 21:27

END OF DAYS 1971– 2001

AN ESCHATOLOGICAL STUDY

CHARLES D. WILLIS, M.D.

EXPOSITION PRESS   NEW YORK

The frontispiece is a rare color picture of a UFO over New Mexico, October, 1957, taken by Ella Fortune, a nurse. Although the object seems to be moving because of the vapor trail, it actually hovered in position. A comparison of the photograph with the visual sighting by Mr. Webb in Arizona in 1953 can lead to the perception that the "cloud" effect is due to the high magnetic field around the object.

EXPOSITION PRESS INC.

50 Jericho Turnpike   Jericho, New York 11753

FIRST EDITION

0-682-47385-5

Dedicated to my wife

SHIRLEY

And the five jewels she has given me

CONTENTS

Preface   9

1. PREPARATION   13

2. ISRAEL: PAST, PRESENT AND FUTURE   21

3. UNIDENTIFIED FLYING OBJECTS   30

4. COMPUTERS, FOOD AND PEOPLE   46

5. THE WORLD CHURCH   49

6. WORLD WAR III PROSPECTS   53

7. THE ANTICHRIST   58

8. THE RAPTURE QUESTION   68

9. JESUS THE CHRIST AND HIS KINGDOM   73

10. A PROBABLE SCENARIO   90

Bibliography   118

And he told them a parable: "Look at the fig tree, and all the trees; as soon as they come out in leaf, you see for yourselves and know that the summer is already near. So also, when you see these things taking place, you know that the kingdom of God is near."—LUKE 21:29-31.

Listen, my friend, to the tick of God's prophetic clock: "About the Time of the End, a body of men will be raised up who will turn their attention to the Prophecies, and insist upon their literal interpretation, in the midst of much clamor and opposition."—ISAAC NEWTON, 1642-1727.

PREFACE

The theme of this work will hopefully help the reader to orient his historical sextant as we sail into the troubled waters of the latter third of the 20th century. A careful analysis of ancient biblical prophecies has been made in relationship to contemporary historical trends. Their growing congruence leads to only one valid conclusion: that the underlying *Realpolitik* of the next thirty years will lead to increasing international centralization and con- solidation of the global human community to be ruled over by a ruthless dictator whose Hitlerian-style regime will finally be crushed by the Second Coming of Christ. A major mystery of the past twenty years, Unidentified Flying Objects, is clearly identified as a reality and a biblical phenomenon with a clear explanation of its meaning. The reason for Earth's dawning Space Age is correlated with this phenomenon. The converging lines of Prophecy and history are, in this study, sharply drawn to a realistic goal in which a thinking person can find real hope amidst the increasing turmoil of the planet Earth. That hope—citizenship in Christ's coming kingdom—is built upon the moral order of the universe, whose reality is as valid as the mathematical principles underlying the physical universe.

C. D. W.

1 PREPARATION

History, to be valuable, should be instructive. The swift passage of current events may seem bewildering to the average onlooker unless one follows Arnold Toynbee's advice to note the "ground swell" of the historical waves. Individual events are usually not important except in certain instances. What is of great value is the observation of long-term trends in the historical process.

Many Christians are convinced that with the reestablishment of Israel in 1948, the latter half of the 20th century constitutes the "eschaton," or end-time, of earth's history which will precede the Second Coming of Christ. This century is therefore pre-eminently a century of prophetic fulfillment, more so than any other since the 1st century saw the coming of the Christ. As the culminating events of the cosmic drama between good and evil begin to formulate, the Christian should be perceptive of them so that he can intelligently redeem the time to further the advancement of the cause of Christ in the best possible manner.

Both Old and New Testaments speak of a climactic end of human history, and biblical teaching is quite clear in identifying this with the Second Coming of Christ. We can begin to perceive as we have entered the Space Age of Earth that "persons in heavenly places" (Eph. 3:10; John 14:2-3[1]) may include the citizens of many worlds like our own except that they have not sinned, who have observed and are observing our follies and long to see Earth's sorry tale brought to an end.

---

[1] Scriptural quotations are from the Revised Standard Version of the Bible, copyright 1946 and 1952 by the Division of Christian Education of the National Council of the Churches of Christ in the U.S.A., and used by permission.

The great sweep of biblical history is what is important in trying to determine the shape of things to come. Some prophetic matters in the Bible have been imperfectly understood (I Cor. 13:9-10), but with the growth of certain global historical developments the perceptive Christian can begin to understand them with growing clarity. It is to the goal of this clarification that this study is directed.

An approach has been made to present certain historical matters in (1) narrative form in which certain facts are presented in chronological order, (2) an attempt to teach the meaning of historical events to provide guidance for individual action and (3) a dynamic concept of certain "end-time" prophetic and historical events in terms of causal and genetic relationships. In this last regard the alert reader and observer of current events will note the convergence of several historical trends that seem to be heading toward a culmination in the Second Coming of Christ (Luke 21:20-28).

Prophecy is of course heady material, and in the past some biblical commentators have gotten carried away with it, causing their more sober brethren to shy from it. However, in the latter half of the 20th century there is one cardinal historical fulfillment that tells the observant believer in the Bible that God has set the prophetic clock in motion, and that is the rise of Israel in 1948. Therefore one can now look with assurance to the conception that the period 1970-2000 is preeminently an age of prophecy.

In conjunction with the arrival of Israel upon the stage of world history we can note the development of some alarming problems in the latter half of this century which can only lead any thinking person to search earnestly for a real meaning to mankind's existence. The real crisis of our age, of course, is a spiritual and moral crisis of Western civilization in which people as individuals no longer believe in the eternal truths of the Christian gospel. The lesson of history is that man was made to live in loving fellowship with God and that when this relationship is broken, certain unhealthy events begin to happen. Persons who have pushed God out of their lives have sought to replace Him with the various political ideologies of our time, all to no avail. The real difficulty, for instance, that the leaders of the Soviet Union face is that neither they nor a good portion of their people believe in God or in "the god that failed—Communism"—hence their ideological crisis. Toynbee has correctly characterized Communism as a Christian heresy, which it is—the "kingdom of god" at the point of a gun! Also, Communist leaders have discovered that morality cannot be implemented by education or social structure as they used to think, and their failure to do so after some fifty years in power is producing strains in the Russian body politic. In the West one sees the governments of various nations attempting to provide a meaning to life. This no earthly government can do, hence the lack of inner peace among the majority of young people. As the world drifts into an increasingly sensate society many of our foremost thinkers are predicting mankind's slide to oblivion. The contending factions of earthpeople will soon render our global spaceship uninhabitable. The prospect of global atomic warfare hangs over our own age like a sword of Damocles. Increasing pollution of our ecological life-support system threatens the very existence of life on earth, and man's greed produces still more destruction of our planetary resources.

The question confronting 20th-century man is, Wherein lie salvation and hope amidst the increasing chaos of the planet Earth? Is there a reality to the supernatural? Since modern physics has shown that over 90 percent of the physical interactions affecting mankind occur in the area of the realities of the electromagnetic spectrum that are not detectable directly by the human sensory organs, moral and personal entities such as the Holy Spirit of which the Bible speaks, become much more plausible to the educated mind. We believe in television waves; although we cannot see them, we do see their effects. Just so do we see the moral "imagery" produced when the Holy Spirit influences individual persons to live better lives as a result of their acceptance of Christ as Lord and Saviour.

The question that is perhaps reasonable to ask in the age we live in is this: Are there any reliable indications that the Bible and its message are true, realistic and accurate, to inform mankind about the future course of history for the planet Earth?

Many problems are impinging upon the collective consciousness of mankind as we near the year 2001! As thinking persons and especially as Christians, we have a basic responsibility to engage in some type of systematic anticipation, some formulation of the future, the most important mode of time. The Bible asserts that it has "models" in its prophetic schemata for the future form of world history. Its models are as deserving of examination as the secular ones now being formulated. Current observers of world society have commented on the global spread of a more or less secular humanism whose values are replacing those of our traditional biblical ones. One perception that is becoming clearer to people is that the optimism of the early part of this century, around 1900, was an unrealistic one. Mankind's illusions about "progress" and building a better world disappeared in the mass futilities of World Wars I and II. Another epochal event in this century that has shattered humanity's earlier optimism is the production of atomic weaponry by China.

How can predictions be evaluated? Without some criteria there can be no judgment. I have offered the biblical model as one which will enable the reader to determine how accurate and reasonable his predictions are. Many men have predicted some events quite accurately, such as H. G. Wells in 1914, who in *The World Set Free* stated that "atomic bombs" would be used in a war in the 1950s. But this prediction is a small one compared to Jesus' jump between the fall and the rise of Israel (A.D. 70-1948) as outlined in Luke 21:23-24.

What is spiritually edifying for men today is to discover by study that the predictions that have been spoken of for so long from the pulpit are finally beginning to become congruent with, and resemble the shape of, world history. Our knowledge of these biblical predictions or prophecies has grown from two sources, namely the increase of basic linguistic and archeological data of the Bible and our great increase in material knowledge, an event in itself predicted in "the time of the end" (Dan. 12:4). The more data one possesses, the more accurate analyses can be made of the knowledge itself. Unfortunately, on our global spaceship wisdom has not extrapolated with knowledge, and by this lack the seeds of destruction can be sown.

In modern times one of the major advances in technology is the invention of the high-speed digital computer. This one invention has set the stage for the rise of a worldwide dictatorship.

Some political theorists are saying that the United States and its 1776 republican principles, essentially a reflection of John Locke, are outmoded in the modern world and that mankind needs a new political theory to undergird government in the 20th century. Where can such a new political theory be found? I am of the opinion that it will be found in the illusionary promises of the united world empire of the Antichrist. The new technology for the acquisition, storage, retrieval, and transmission of data via computer technology has made it possible to create a world state which can control and locate every individual in the world with incredible electronic swiftness.

The problem of controlling or modifying "human nature" will become more urgent and pressing as the global compaction of population grows worse. The global world empire will see behavior manipulations on a scale never before attempted in human society, and all rationalized by the need to have "peace." This control will not be successful, since totalitarian regimes carry within themselves the seeds of their own destruction.

One of the phenomena of this latter era of the 20th century is the increasing secularization of the church. Even secular thinkers are envisaging a synthesis of a one-world religion as a possible development.

A noted anthropologist of our time has commented that for the first time in her experience, seemingly *all* the youth of the world are in revolt against organized authority structures. The reason for the universal rebellion will be developed later in this study. The conventions of society have been torn so severely that never in our lifetime will we see life morally as it was in the days of our fathers, when a man's word was his bond.

We have already noted in the 1960s invasions of privacy by governmental institutions. These will increase, and some of the areas now considered private will yield to governmental control in the years to come. Global telecommunications will be a powerful tool in the hands of the world government.

The future of international society is one of deep concern

to conscientious statesmen who vainly try to modify evil human nature within political systems. The growth of the United Nations, while it yet is fragile in the exertion of beneficial power, will in time be a basis for the creation of a world empire, since there are many signs that the exclusively "American" world system is in a process of decay and in a relative decline in international politics. Certain historical trends can be distinguished by thoughtful analysis of the probable course of international events in the next thirty years. Greater European and Western civilization cohesiveness will develop, primarily for economic reasons. Tension between the West and the Eastern European community will decrease.

With China seeking to replace Russia's influence in the African-Arabian sphere of concern, major conflict may break out in the late 1970s. As an ideology Communism will continue to decline.

Certain types of prediction are derivative from perfect data, and few of us have that kind of information. However, the data from which this study is drawn, while necessarily not perfect, has the advantage of the use of the Bible, a collection of books which has survived the skeptics' inquiry over thousands of years to rest in still-current belief in the hearts of millions of persons.

Two major biblical prophetic concepts are necessarily to be understood if the reader is to obtain the most from this study. The first is the prophetic model of the "seventy weeks of years" found in Daniel 9. Basically stated, it predicts and develops the following theme:

> There are Seventy Weeks of years referred to in Daniel's prophecy (Dan. 9:20-27). During these seventy weeks of seven years each Daniel prophesied that Israel's national chastisement would be terminated and the nation reestablished in "everlasting righteousness" (vs. 24). In Daniel's vision the weeks are divided into three parts, seven weeks equalling forty nine years; sixty two weeks totaling 434 years; one week equalling seven years (Dan. 9:25-27). In the seven weeks or forty nine years Jerusalem was to be reconstructed in "troubled times." This was brought to pass as recorded in the books of Ezra-Nehemiah. In the sixty-two weeks or 434 years Messiah was to come at

His first advent (vs. 25), fulfilled in Messiah's birth and his being "cut off but not for Himself" at the crucifixion. The date of Christ's crucifixion is evidently not specified except that it is to be after the "three score and two weeks." The city was to be destroyed by "the people of the prince that shall come." This was fulfilled by the Romans under Titus in A.D. 70. Verse 27, by many commentators, is connected immediately with the events of the first advent. However many premillennialists place it in the end time and between verse 26 and 27. In this extended period they place the church age as an era unrevealed in O.T. prophecy (Matt. 13:11-17; Eph. 3:1-10). During this time it is maintained that the mysteries of the kingdom of heaven (Matt. 13:1-50) and the outcalling of the church are consummated. According to this view, the church age will terminate at an unspecified moment and will usher in Daniel's seventieth week. The personage of verse 27 thus under this interpretation, is identical with the little horn of Daniel 7, who will make a covenant with the Jews to restore their Judaic ritual for one week—seven years. In the middle of the week he will break the covenant and fulfill Daniel 12:11 and II Thessalonians 2:3-11. This interpretation views verse 27 as dealing with the last three and one half years of the Great Tribulation (Matt. 24:15-28). This era is connected with the "time of trouble" spoken of by Daniel (Dan. 12:1) with the "abomination of desolation" (Matt. 24:15) and with the "hour of trial" (Rev. 3:10)[2]

As will be seen in this study, I have concluded that the "premillennial end-time" interpretation is correct and fits the developing picture of world history best.

The other basic prophetic scheme necessary for understanding this study is also found in the Book of Daniel. The story as it unfolds in Daniel 1 and 2 is basically that the king of Babylon had a most unusual dream. Of all the educated "wise men" at court, only Daniel, a Jewish youth of noble birth, could interpret the meaning of his dream to the king. The dream is most interesting, since it outlines a general scheme of world history that will come to pass from Daniel's day until the close of the present age. Daniel lived and worked in the 5th century B.C., a discouraging time,

---

[2] Merrill F. Unger, *Unger's Bible Handbook* (Chicago, Moody Press, 1966), p. 1000. Used by permission.

since he had seen his nation Israel crushed and destroyed by Nebuchadnezzar, king of Babylon, who had taken him with many of his people captive to Babylon after the fall of Jerusalem. Yet in the midst of national disaster Daniel was faithful to his God, who rewarded him accordingly.

In the dream interpreted by Daniel, the king saw a great image symbolizing the political realities and instrumentalities of the Gentile world powers to come.

Dan. 2:31-35:

> *"You saw, O King, and behold, a great image. This image, mighty and of exceeding brightness, stood before you, and its appearance was frightening. The head of this image was of fine gold, its breast and arms of silver, its belly and thighs of bronze, its legs of iron and partly of clay. As you looked, a stone was cut out by no human hand, and it smote the image on its feet of iron and clay, and broke them in pieces; then the iron, the clay, the bronze, the silver, and the gold, all together were broken in pieces, and became like the chaff of the summer threshing floors; and the wind carried them away, so that not a trace of them could be found. But the stone that struck the image became a great mountain and filled the whole earth."*

The explanation of this vision was that Nebuchadnezzar's Babylonian kingdom of gold would give way to the silver of Persia, to be followed by the bronze of Greece under Alexander the Great. And after Greece would rise the greatest of ancient empires, that of the iron majesty of Rome, founder of Western civilization which would not pass away until the coming of stone—the Messianic kingdom.

That this final kingdom would be a success and accomplished by God's direct intervention in human history is the teaching of this biblical passage. While briefly sketched here, these matters have been dealt with at length by other authors. The West still stands with its heritage of Greek-Roman culture, although in decline, as observed by many historians. This decline, however, precedes the dawn of a new age for the planet Earth, that of the Millennial Kingdom.

2 ISRAEL: PAST, PRESENT AND FUTURE

In effecting the plan of salvation through the Christ, God had to select a Chosen People to serve as a communicative channel in order to develop the plan which would give man a second chance to live the eternal life he was originally destined to fulfill. If God had not done so, the cries of the weeping children of earth would have echoed unanswered throughout the universe. And the inhabitants of other worlds would have been dismayed. But God so loved us that He sent His Son that through Him we might have eternal life (John 3:16).

The special vehicle of communication that God chose was the seed of Abraham, the Jews, a people who have amazingly survived the wreck of many a civilization for over four thousand years. Abraham was the man that God chose as the father of a special group of people in the world to effect the great manifestation of His steadfast love for mankind. From Isaac, the son of the promise, eventually came the twelve tribes of Israel. The request by God for Abraham to sacrifice his son as an offering may be seen as a subtle symbolism of the fact that God would effect man's salvation through the eventual sacrifice of His Son, the Christ-Person, on the hill of Calvary.

Under the protection of Joseph, the brother so cruelly sold into slavery but who remained faithful to God, the beginnings of the nation of Israel, formulated as the sons of Jacob, gathered into Egypt at the time of the seven-year famine. Joseph ruled the land of Egypt in Pharaoh's name; after him, however, the Hebrews fell upon hard times as they were enslaved by the Egyptians. After many years of bitter bondage God provided a leader who was unique in world history—Moses, prince of Egypt, shepherd, and later leader of his people in the exodus under Rameses II. Leading his people forth into the wilderness of Sinai, Moses brought them to a spectacular confrontation with God himself. Under the shadow of this brooding mountain were delivered laws and instructions: an agreement—a covenant—for the people of Israel to guide them in their life's pathway. Promises were given to Israel that faithfulness to the covenant would bring blessing, and departure from it would cause sorrow and unhappiness.

Of all the religious ordinances a few can be mentioned to highlight the significance of this communicative experience with God. Basically, all the various sacrificial ordinances pointed to one lesson: that through a propitiatory act, a sacrifice, man was reconciled to God and restored to fellowship with Him. These ordinances were in themselves only "types," or lessons, of the reality that was to come when Christ, the "Lamb of God," would come and effect the reality of the atonement.

Another part of the laws of ancient Israel was the institution of the Year of Jubilee. While this might seem at first glance to be a relatively minor aspect of the Mosaic code, the reader will perceive later on in this study that it contains a profoundly significant symbolism that will help us to understand the history of the latter third of the 20th century. The Year of Jubilee, or literally the "year of the ram's horn" in Hebrew (Lev. 25:28; 25:10-13), portrays an interesting symbolism in that this final year in a cycle of fifty years consisting of seven sabbatical year periods, or forty-nine years plus one year was the Year of Liberty (Ezek. 46:17), during which slaves were freed and family property previously sold was restored to the original owners. It was therefore a time of rejoicing for the people and a sacred time during which the land was rested from its agricultural use and the people of God sought to commune with Him in a more intimate relationship.

When Moses died, the leadership of Israel passed to Joshua, who led Israel into the promised land and to the establishment of a nation that was destined to formulate the course of human history more than any other nation. A fitting climax to Joshua's life and a tribute to his moral leadership is the statement that the people "served the Lord all the days of Joshua."

For the next few hundred years Israel was ruled by judges in a somewhat loosely confederated commonwealth. The story is one of sin and apostasy bringing foreign oppression followed by repentance and deliverance. The basic difficulty then as now was with mankind's idolatry.

Finally the people of Israel called for a king. The first king was Saul, who began well but finally with presumption attempted to perform priestly roles for which God had not selected him. His failure to fully obey God led to rejection of him as king. During this time a young shepherd was faithfully tending his flocks in Bethlehem until one day the aged prophet Samuel appeared and anointed him King of Israel. The reign of David ushered in an outstanding period of Jewish history. David was a superb military leader whose courage in early youth was exemplified by his slaying the giant Philistine, Goliath. His last attainments were spiritual ones. He wrote songs and poems for private and public worship, and Israel came to a position of honor and blessing with God it had never attained before. David sinned grievously in committing adultery and murder as regards Uriah's wife, Bathsheba. Although repentant under God's rebuke he suffered punishment as a result of this sin.

The height of Israel's glory as a nation in the first millennium B.C. was perhaps reached under the reign of Solomon, the son of David. Fabled for his wisdom, Solomon brought new prosperity to Israel and a peaceful reign of some forty years.

During these years promises were made by God that the Davidic line would for all time constitute the royal house of Israel (II Sam. 7:4-16; Ps. 89:3; 4:29, 34-37). Therefore it was inevitable that the Messiah-King of Israel who would eventually reign over Israel and all the earth would come of the royal seed of David; so the lineage of Christ is carefully described (Luke 1:31-33) and the kingdom promise to Him reaffirmed.

Subsequent to Solomon, through many centuries, Israel was ruled by a succession of kings, some good like Hezekiah, others evil like Manasseh, and the kingdom was torn in two. Finally God chastened Israel, and the people were dispersed for seventy years (Jer. 25:11), until repentance had prepared them for a restoration.

In the providence of God, Cyrus, king of Persia, allowed the Jews to return to Israel and assisted them in doing so. Ezra and Nehemiah were at that time leaders in this movement and wrote the books that bear their names and a record of the times in which they lived. So Israel was restored; and the Old Testament closes in Malachi with the promise "Behold, I will send you Elijah the prophet before the great and terrible day of the Lord comes." Jesus pointed out, and Christians believe, that this was a symbolic prediction of John the Baptist, who considered himself a forerunner of Jesus.

There now developed a scriptural silence for some four hundred years between the Testaments. To fill this void one must needs have recourse to secular historians. During the few centuries before Christ, Israel enjoyed some degree of independence but lost it later under Syrian rule, when she was conquered by Antiochus the Great. Following him, Antiochus Epiphanes arose and he, in his efforts to stamp out Judaism entirely, subjected the Jews to unspeakable persecution. Antiochus was a prophetic "type," or forerunner, of the Antichrist.

This tyranny was overthrown by the heroic Maccabees, who carved out about a hundred years of independence for Israel. Their deeds are celebrated in the Jewish Feast of Lights, also called Hannukah, usually in December of each year. Finally, in 63 B.C., Rome conquered Judea and made it a Roman province. With the incorporation of Judea into the unitary civilization of Rome, the stage was set for the most decisive event in human history—the coming of the Messiah of Israel, Jesus Christ. His life, teaching, and atoning death were God's ultimate answer to the problem of evil, which if it had not been dealt with could have eventually destroyed the entire universe.

With the death, resurrection, and ascension of Jesus the fate of Israel assumed a twofold pattern. The one was that of the birth of the early Christian church, which evolved from its beginning as a sect of the Nazarenes within Judaism. It soon spread in obedience to the command of Jesus to encompass all nations. The other was the dispersion but preservation of the ethnic seed of Abraham for a future role in history (Rom. 11:1-36). Israel was

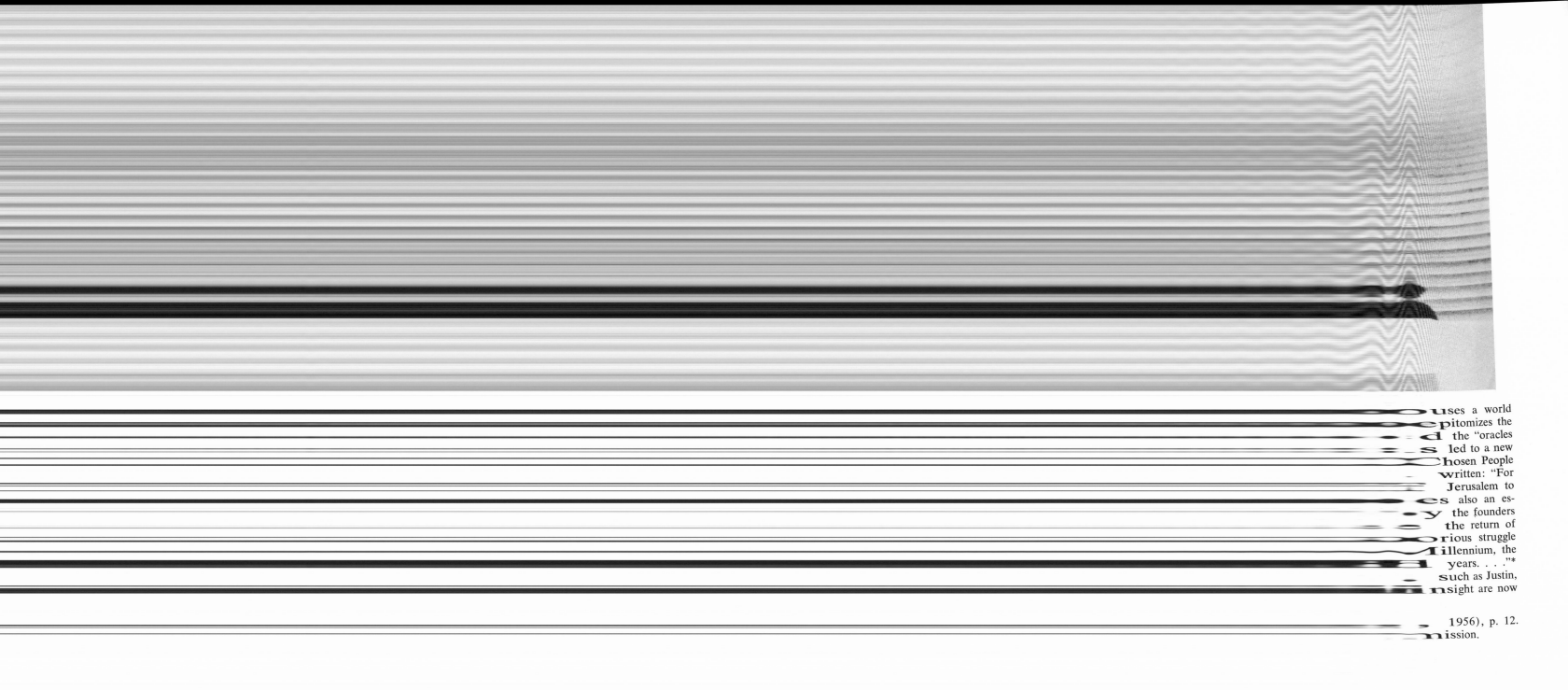

26

dispersed throughout
words in Luke 21:20
years the Chosen Pe
being the recipient a
understanding of rati
participated in this p
they are really imbu
commission toward th
for which they shall h
　Many Christian
that before the end-tim
of Christ a cardinal hi
of the nation of Israel
ever be returned to th
idea to some people in
tures were wiser than th

　　The Jews shall be
　they are now scattere
　. . . the Lord Christ
　also be acknowledge
　OWEN, 1673.

　　Israel is now blotte
　are scattered far and
　rivers of the earth.
　will be a native gover
　of a body politic . . .

Another voice from th
of Israel's restoration wa
can Colonial minister wh
rise again as a nation an
cede the Second Coming
establish His kingdom.
　In testimony before the
July 9, 1947, the Chief
stated:

　　In accordance with
　return to Palestine befo

should be a part of Palestine. Only then, after the return of
the Jews of Palestine, in accordance with the tradition the
Messiah will arrive.

Christians are in complete agreement with the good Rabbi. The beginning of the historical process which has resulted in the rise of Israel began in the 1880s when the first wave of Jewish immigrants returned to Palestine. In 1896 Herzl published his Zionist manifesto and gave added impetus to the return. In 1917 the smashing of the Ottoman Empire opened the door for more Jewish immigration. Finally in 1948, amidst blood, sweat, and tears, the new state of Israel came into being. In 1956 Israel was threatened by encircling Arabs and won a speedy victory. In 1967 Israel again faced a serious threat to her existence and again achieved an astounding victory, in six days. The swift annihilating air strikes against the Arab air forces were spectacular in their effect. They were quickly followed by a desert tank-infantry assault in the Sinai that was a classic of tactical warfare. To crown Israel's victory, Jerusalem was completely secured, thus no longer being "trodden down by the Gentiles" (Luke 21:24).

In a recent book Israel's Foreign Minister, the brilliant and loquacious Abba Eban, asks, "Where do we go from here?" It is to help answer that question that this study has been prepared; and the answer lies in a correct amalgamation of both Old Testament and New Testament prophecies.

The future destiny of Israel is seen similarly by both Jewish rabbinical authorities and Christian prophetic interpreters. A possible failure to be wholly consecrated to God's will may bring a sequence of retribution in the form of cataclysmic trial during the Great Tribulation conceived of unwittingly by Jewish writers as the "birth pangs of the Messiah," to be followed by repentance of a remnant of Israel who will survive and enter into the redemptive Messianic kingdom—a small group of the pious, righteous, and humble among the sons of Israel (Rev. 7:1-8).

Since Israel is reestablished as a result of God's sovereign will, she will not pass away. At the same time no real peace will come to the Mideast area. The gradual growth of Russian power and influence in the area is viewed by some as a definite fulfillment of the "King of the North" prophecy, which may refer to the USSR directly or to one of its minions, such as Syria. There are some indications of an attempted invasion of Israel by Russia, which will end in disaster—for the Russians.

As will be developed later in this study, there are some indications in prophecy that the Antichrist world dictator will offer to make a treaty, or "covenant," with Israel and guarantee her safety. He may be able to do this as the leader of a pan-Arabic federation as well as in his role of world dictator (Dan. 9:24-27). If Israel accepts, a period of pseudo peace will prevail in the first half of the seven years allotted to his reign.

However, the Antichrist will, like Antiochus Epiphanes and Caligula, demand that both the world population and the Jews worship his image and himself as a god. This demand most of the world will obey, except those who call upon the name of Jesus Christ and suffer martyrdom (Rev. 7:1-17). Israel will refuse his demand also, and the Antichrist will seek to destroy her. In Israel's darkest hour the Messiah will come and the Davidic kingdom will be founded.

Subsequent to this deliverance Israel will be the leading nation of the world. The global society of this planet will be completely transformed by righteousness, and in the effecting of this change the seed of Abraham will have a foremost role, as so long promised. The past historical failures of the Jewish people have been matched by Christians in the church, so that neither one is in a position to offer criticism to the other. In spite of a major failure to recognize the Messiah when He first came, the Jewish people have done a heroic job over the millenniums in preserving for mankind the "oracles of God" and have been the vehicle of God's plan of salvation for this world. We owe them much, and only God can judge them.

The "eagles" of Israel that destroyed the Arab air forces in a smashing early-morning attack in June, 1967, at which time the promise of Deut. 20:1-4 was fulfilled. The God of their fathers went before the men of Israel to give them an astounding victory, and to smite the House of Egypt.

3 UNIDENTIFIED FLYING OBJECTS

In the past twenty years a global phenomenon has appeared in the skies of this planet which has puzzled and intrigued those who have studied it. This UFO phenomenon, has in the process, aroused a certain amount of controversy.

Although the modern period of the UFO phenomenon dates from Kenneth Arnold's sighting of "flying saucers" in 1947 over the Mount Rainier range, ancient records indicate that UFOs have been with man for a long time.

Secular records include some of the following, which may indicate that the earth has been visited by intelligent extraterrestrial beings for many centuries. During the reign of Thutmose III, Pharaoh of Egypt, 1504-1450 B.C., there are records of the "fire circles" appearing in the skies over Egypt. In the times of the Roman Empire, 99 B.C., "when C. Murius and L. Valerius were consuls, in Tarquinia . . . (50 miles north of Rome), towards sunset, a round object like a globe, or round or circular shield (*orbis clypei*) took its path in the sky, from west to east." In A.D. 1290 a flat, round, shining silvery object (discus) flew over the abbey of Begelend, England, and was seen by the abbot and his monks, causing considerable consternation. Many reports exist of an "airship" appearing in 1897 over the United States in several localities, including San Francisco.

Numerous other examples of the UFO phenomenon down through the ages have been collected. Some of these sightings were similar to modern ones but of course were interpreted within the psychology of the times. Perhaps the best summary of the modern evidence regarding UFOs can be found in the report of the Committee on Science and Astronautics of the U.S. Congress, dated July 20, 1968, and entitled "UFO Symposium."

Two of the most reliable sighting reports are included in this study. They serve to indicate that unless one wishes to postulate a global psychosis the UFO phenomenon is very real and demands explanation from any thinking person.

The following UFO sighting was made by Rev. W. B. Gill, a teacher and missionary of the Anglican church, on June 26-27, 1959. It is valuable not only because it comes from a morally credible source but also because it is a multiple-witness sighting. The site was Boiannai, New Guinea. While Gill watched along with some thirty-nine other witnesses, he saw three aerial disk-shaped forms appear and hover above him at an altitude of about 350 feet. The object that was seen the best was described as disk-shaped, and seen on the upper deck of it were four humanoid beings. They seemed to be working on or about some object on the deck. The beings on the aerial disk waved in response to arm movements of Gill and his party on the ground. Some of the witnesses reported seeing glowing portholes in the object, which finally left the scene about half an hour after it had appeared. The number of witnesses, their moral caliber, and the details make this an exceptionally good sighting, one of the most accurate on record.

Another very reliable sighting occurred at Haneda Airport, Tokyo, Japan, in the summer of 1952 at about 11:30 P.M. Two control-tower operators at Haneda AFB saw a brilliant light to the northeast which seemed to drift closer. They went up into the tower and got a good look at the light with 7 x 50 binoculars, it was also viewed by the two tower operators they were relieving. It appeared as a circular-shaped light which was the upper portion of a large round, dark shape about four times the diameter of the light itself.

One of the operators called a nearby radar site and asked if they had an unidentified target on their scopes. They did, and a comparison of information over the telephone revealed that the control-tower operators and the radar operators were observing the same object simultaneously.

A few minutes after midnight an F-94 plane was scrambled from nearby Johnson AFB and came into the area. The ground controller was able to direct the F-94 so that it went south of Yokohama, up Tokyo Bay, and was brought in behind the UFO. The radar operator in the rear seat of the F-94 called in to the tower that he had a radar lock on the object. The lockon was held for over a minute as the ground controller observed both F-94 and UFO make a·turn and come toward the ground radar site. The UFO then pulled away from the F-94 in a swift acceleration. The F-94 then left the area; the UFO returned and was observed again both visually by the tower operators and electronically by the ground radar station until it finally departed a few minutes later. The reliability of this particular report is of the highest caliber, since it includes visual sighting by highly qualified aeronautical personnel and multiple radar-image confirmation.

These and other such sightings can only lead to the conclusion that the UFO phenomenon is very real. It is being reported from every continent upon the face of the earth. Within the past two years reports of combined visual-radar sightings in the USSR have been published.

The number of sightings of unusual aerial phenomena by reliable persons, such as pilots, meteorologists, and astronomers, over the last twenty years has led responsible persons to reach such conclusions as these:

> *I am aware that hundreds of military and airline pilots, airport personnel, astronomers, missile trackers and other competent observers have reported sightings of Unidentified Flying Objects. I am also aware that many of these UFOs have been observed maneuvering in formation, and that many were simultaneously being tracked by radar. It is my opinion that: The UFOs reported by competent observers are devices under intelligent control. Their speeds, maneuvers and other technical evidence prove them superior to any aircraft or space devices now produced on earth. These UFOs are interplanetary devices systematically observing the Earth, either manned or under remote control or both. Information on UFOs, including sightings reports, has been and still is being officially withheld.—* COLONEL J. J. BRYAN, *III, USAF Retired.*

> *. . . my own present opinion based on two years of careful study is that UFOs are probably extraterrestrial devices engaged in something that might very tentatively be termed "surveillance."—*JAMES E. MCDONALD, *Physicist, University of Arizona.*

The hypothesis that UFOs originate in other worlds, that they are flying craft from planets other than earth, merits the most serious examination.—FELIX ZIGEL, Sc.D. *Moscow Aviation Institute, USSR.*

Over the past twenty years a vast amount of evidence has been accumulating that bears on the existence of UFOs. Most of this is little known to the general public or to most scientists. But on the basis of the data and ordinary rules of evidence as would be applied in civil or criminal courts, the physical reality of UFOs has been proved beyond a reasonable doubt. —JAMES A. HARDER, *Professor, Civil Engineering, University of California.*

Other opinions and observations from equally reliable persons are available to anyone who will investigate the serious UFO literature.

The alert Christian should of course be keenly aware of the world he lives in and be quick to perceive historical trends that bear on the meaning of his own Christian experience, the church, and the outlines of God's plan for the history of the world. Several questions come to mind about the UFO phenomenon. Is it a biblical phenomenon? If so, what is its meaning in this modern period of time, and how does it fit into the prophetic end-time schemata?

Several authors, both secular and religious, have referred to the experience of Ezekiel in the first few chapters of his book as being the earliest recorded visitation by extraterrestrial intelligent beings to this world. However, other students of the problem have pointed out that a complete study of the "pillar of cloud" that led Israel from Egypt leads to the conclusion that it was some type of aerodynamic vehicle. The section on the Old Testament in Rev. Mr. Downing's book develops this rather well, as does also Paul Misraki of France. The biblical references that are of interest to us in deciding the question are listed below. A few selected ones will be examined in detail.

Ex. 13:21-22; 14:19-20, 24; 16:10; 19:16-18; 24:9-11, 15-18; 33:9-11; 34:5; 40:34-38; Num. 9:15-23; 10:11-12,34; 11:25; 12:1-9; Deut. 31:14-23; II Kings 2:1-12; Neh. 9:12,19; Ps. 78:14; 99:7; 104:3; 105:39; Isa. 4:2-6; Ezek. 1:1-28; 2:1-

The Mysterious Flying Light that Hovered over St. Mary's College, Oakland, and then started for San Francisco. It is exactly that described by Sacramentans, and similar to the cut published a few days ago in "The Call" from a description furnished by one who saw it.

Engraving published in the *San Francisco Call* in November, 1896. Donald Hanlon, who has catalogued more than 150 sightings for the 1896-97 wave, reports that the object was seen throughout the United States and became popularly known as "The Airship." It was highly maneuverable and was equipped with powerful lights; it landed several times and was definitely not the work of local craftsmen.

From Jacques & Janine Vallee, *Challenge to Science: The UFO Enigma* (Chicago: Regnery, 1966).

10; 3:1-15; 11:22; Dan. 7:13-14; Matt. 17:5; 24:30-31; 26:64; Mark 9:2-8; 13:26; 14:62; Luke 9:28-36; 21:27; Acts 1:9-11; I Cor. 10:1; I Thess. 4:14-17; Rev. 1:7; 11:12.

Jesus made a point of stating that He would return to this planet in a "cloud." To elucidate this rather cryptic statement, one must go to the Old Testament. It can be noted firstly, however, that in the classic passage on the ascension of Christ, Acts 1:9-12, four pertinent Greek words are used. One is *eperthe,* meaning a lifting up as in referring to a sail being hoisted (Acts 27:40). In verse 9 He was "received" up by the cloud, the Greek here being *hypeleben,* meaning as if the cloud "supported" Him. Another word, *analemphtheis,* is used in Acts 1:11 and is translated "received up." This word is also used in Acts 20:13-14, where it refers to "boarding" a ship. All of this argues that the kind of cloud that took Jesus away from this planet was something quite different from the gaseous visible body of fine droplets of water dispersed in the atmosphere that we commonly refer to. The data is now sufficient to formulate the postulate that Jesus left this world and will return to it in some type of technologically superior spaceship. The technology of these matters has not been sophisticated enough for mankind to clearly understand the reality of the Scripture until modern times.

A well-known American biblical scholar, Rev. John P. Walvoord, echoes other men when he declares the theophany of the angel of Jehovah in the Old Testament time to have been the preincarnate Christ. This is not to say that in a humanoid form God is limited to such an anthropomorphic theophany. God can reveal Himself in a form or not as He wills. However, it can be argued that when He does, certain physical-spatial boundaries are usefully utilized. That God did in O.T. times thus exhibit Himself in a humanoid form is always surprising to some people, so that the Scripture is quoted here directly.

Ex. 24:9-11:

> *"Then Moses and Aaron, Nadab and Abihu, and seventy of the elders of Israel went up, and they saw the God of Israel; and there was under his feet as it were a pavement of sapphire stone, like the very heaven for clearness. And he did not lay*

his hand on the chief men of the people of Israel; they beheld God and ate and drank."

Ezek. 1:26:

"And above the firmament over their heads there was the likeness of a throne, in appearance like sapphire; and seated above the likeness of a throne was a likeness as it were of a human form."

At the time of God's visitation to Ezekiel he saw "a wheel upon the earth beside the living creatures . . ." (Ezek. 1:15). His description of wheels and "rims . . . full of eyes. . . ." Sounds like a discoid flying saucer with portholes!

We notice several phenomenological details about the "pillar of cloud" that led Israel by day and had the "appearance of fire by night" (Num 9:16) that can lead us to suspect that there was more to this pillar than met the eye. In this case it is best to let the Scripture speak for itself.

Ex. 14:19-20,24:

"Then the angel of God who went before the host of Israel moved and went behind them . . . coming between the host of Egypt and the host of Israel. . . . And in the morning watch the Lord in the pillar of fire and of cloud looked down upon the host of the Egyptians. . . ."

Ex. 24:18:

"And Moses entered the cloud, and went up on the mountain. . . ."

Ex. 33:9-11:

"When Moses entered the tent, the pillar of cloud would descend and stand at the door of the tent, and the Lord would speak with Moses. And when all the people saw the pillar of cloud standing at the door of the tent, all the people would rise up and worship, every man at his tent door. Thus the Lord used to speak to Moses face to face, as a man speaks to his friend."

Ex. 34:5:

"And the Lord descended in the cloud and stood with him [Moses] there, and proclaimed the name of the Lord."

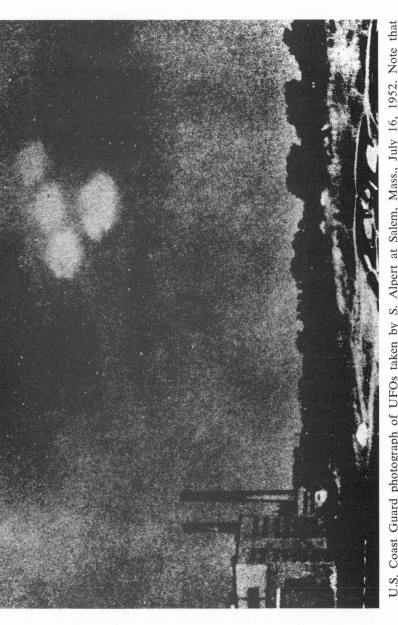

U.S. Coast Guard photograph of UFOs taken by S. Alpert at Salem, Mass., July 16, 1952. Note that these "clouds" are all of the same size and in formation. There are many reports now available in UFO literature of sightings of "clouds" that do not act like clouds at all. "Behold, he is coming with the clouds, and every eye will see him . . . and all tribes of the earth. . . . Even so. Amen" (Rev. 1:7).

Num. 11:24-25:

> *"So Moses went out and told the people the words of the Lord; and he gathered seventy men of the elders of the people, and placed them round about the tent. Then the Lord came down in the cloud and spoke to him, and took some of the spirit that was upon him and put it upon the seventy elders. . . ."*

Num. 12:5-10:

> *"And the Lord came down in a pillar of cloud, and stood at the door of the tent, and called Aaron and Miriam; and they both came forward. And he said, "Hear my words: If there is a prophet among you, I the Lord make myself known to him in a vision, I speak with him in a dream. Not so with my servant Moses; he is entrusted with all my house. With him I speak mouth to mouth, clearly, and not in dark speech; and he beholds the form of the Lord. Why then were you not afraid to speak against my servant Moses?" . . . and when the cloud removed from over the tent. . . ."*

Traditional echoes of this exodus experience of Israel are found in Ps. 99:7 and Ps. 104:3, among others. When one notes that Moses goes "into" the "cloud" (Ex. 24:18) and compares this with the description of Moses and Elijah on a later trip to the planet Earth, when they are seen to have "entered the cloud" (Luke 9:34), one can only conclude that some type of space vehicle is being described.

Down through the ages there have been UFO sightings which are obviously not due to natural phenomena. One that commands our attention was made in A.D. 1322 by one Robert of Reading. The researcher in this case is Harold T. Wilkins.

> *In the first hour of the night of November 4th, there was seen in the sky over Uxbridge, England, a pillar of fire the size of a small boat, pallid, and livid in color. It rose from the south, crossed the sky with a slow and grave motion and went north. Out of the front of the pillar, a fervent red flame burst forth with great beams of light. Its speed increased (it can be noted that meteors do not accelerate noticeably), and it flew thro' the air. . . .*

Several modern-day UFO sightings have been made of huge cylindrical forms surrounded by cloudlike formation, often vertical.

A primitive people would have called such an object a "pillar."
Two modern-day cylindrical type UFO sightings are given below.
October 17, 1952, Orloron, France:

*The weather was superb, with a sky of cloudless blue. About
12.50 P.M. Mr. Yves Prigent, the General Superintendent of
the Oloron High School, was preparing to sit down to lunch in
his apartment on the second floor of the school. With him were
Mme. Prigent, a schoolmistress and their three children. The
windows of the apartment opened on a wide panorama to the
north of the town. Jean-Yves Prigent was at the window and
was just being called to the table, when he cried out, "Oh Papa,
come look, its fantastic!"*

*The whole family joined him at the window and this is M.
Prigent's account of what they saw.*

*In the north, a cottony cloud of strange shape was floating
against the blue sky. Above it, a long narrow cylinder, apparently inclined at a 45 degree angle, was slowly moving in a
straight line toward the southwest. I estimated its altitude as
2 or 3 kilometers. The object was whitish, non-luminous and
very distinctly defined. A sort of plume of white smoke was
escaping from its upper end. At some distance in front of the
cylinder about thirty other objects were following the same
trajectory. To the naked eye they appeared as featureless balls
resembling puffs of smoke. But with the help of opera glasses
it was possible to make out a central red sphere surrounded
by a sort of yellowish ring inclined at an angle.[1]*

October 27, 1952, Gaillac, France:

*At about 5 P.M. Mme. Daures, living on Toulouse Road in
Gaillac, was induced to go out into her farmyard by a noisy
commotion among the chickens. Thinking her flock threatened
by a hawk, she raised her eyes to the sky and saw there exactly
what the Oloronese had seen ten days before. Mme. Daures
called her son. Then two neighbors, then a third. But already
many residents of Gaillac were scanning the skies, among them
two under-officers of the police brigade—in all, about a hundred
known witnesses. All gave the same description, which is
rigorously identical to that of Oloron. Long plumed cylinder
inclined at 45 degrees, progressing slowly to the southeast in
the midst of a score of objects which shone in the sun and*

---

[1] André Michel, *The Truth About Flying Saucers* (S. G. Phillips, 1956),
pp. 153-54. Used by permission of the publisher.

*flew two by two in a rapid zigzag. The only difference is that
here some pairs of the smaller objects occasionally descended
quite low to an altitude estimated by the observers as 300-400
meters. The spectacle lasted for about 20 minutes before the
cigar and its saucers disappeared over the horizon.*[2]

These reports are representative of other, similar ones of cylindrical UFOs. One can conclude that the "pillar of cloud" was indeed some type of space vehicle. There are quite a few biblical
references to the existence of an extraterrestrial civilization, such
as Gen. 6:2-4, Job 1:6-7, John 14:2-3, Eph. 3:10, and Heb. 13:2.
In an excellent study by Walter Sullivan, *We Are Not Alone,*
some of the evidences from the field of astronomy have been clearly outlined for the support of the idea that there is very likely
intelligent life on other worlds throughout the universe. The arrival
of earth's own Space Age has enabled mankind to accept this idea
with more readiness than in prior centuries of human history. In
1968 people all over the world were thrilled when America's astronauts circled the moon, and the fact that their message from space
glorified their Creator during the Christmas season was felt to be
spiritually significant. The soaring triumph of America's astronauts
in landing on the moon in the summer of 1969 verified the probable reality of interplanetary travel for the people of earth.

Recorded Jul. 2, 1963 L.D.

"Brook Hill,"
Richmond 27, Va.
June 30, 1963

Maj. Donald E. Keyhoe, USMC, Ret.
  Director, National Investigations Committee
  on Aerial Phenomena,
1536 Connecticut Ave., NW.,
Washington 6, D.C.

Dear Major Keyhoe:

  I am aware that hundreds of military and airline pilots,
airport personnel, astronomers, missile trackers and other com-

---

[2] *Ibid.,* pp. 155-56.

petent observers have reported sightings of UFOs (Unidentified Flying Objects). I am also aware that many of these UFOs have been observed maneuvering in formation, and that many were tracked by radar simultaneously. It is my opinion that:

The UFOs reported by competent observers are devices under intelligent control.

Their speeds, maneuvers and other technical evidence prove them superior to any aircraft or space devices now produced on earth.

These UFOs are interplanetary devices systematically observing the earth, either manned or under remote control, or both.

Information on UFOs, including sighting reports, has been and is still being officially withheld. This policy is dangerous, especially since mistaken identification of UFOs as a secret Russian attack might accidentally set off war. Unless the policy is changed, a Congressional investigation should be held to reduce or eliminate this and other dangers.

Very truly yours,

J. Bryan, III,
Colonel, USAFR (Ret.)

Colonel Bryan is a former Special Assistant to the Secretary of the Air Force (1952-1953) and was later assigned to the staff of General Lauris Norstad, then Supreme Allied Commander, Europe.

At least two UFO sightings have been made by competent persons that help to clarify exactly what Jesus meant when He said He would return to this planet "in a cloud with power" (Luke 21:27). In 1956 a Russian pilot on ice patrol over the island of Greenland reported:

> . . . *we dropped down from the clouds to fair weather and suddenly noticed an unknown flying craft moving on our portside parallel to our course. It looked very much like a large pearl-colored lens with wavy, pulsating edges. . . . When we changed our course, the unknown flying machine followed suit and moved parallel at our speed . . . the unknown craft sharply altered its course, sped ahead of us and rose quickly*

An excellent UFO photograph made by an Oregon farmer, Paul Trent, on May 11, 1950. The configuration of the vehicle is exactly similar to that of one photographed in France in 1954. Some UFO sightings have combined visual and radar contact, rendering them highly reliable.

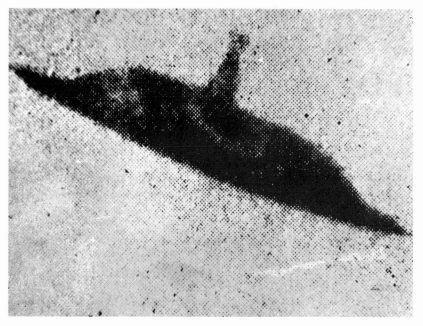

A UFO whose configuration is strikingly similar to the one photographed by Paul Trent in 1950. This one was taken near Rouen, France, four years later, in 1954.

*until it disappeared in the blue sky. . . . It flew at what seemed
to us an impossible speed.*[3]

Another sighting report by Wells A. Webb, a chemist with an
M. Sc. degree from the University of California, also enables us
to get a clue to just what Jesus meant by the term "cloud." Webb's
sighting, made near Yuma, Arizona, in 1953, is described in the
congressional report as follows:

*. . . his attention was drawn to the sky to the north by some
low flying jet aircraft. Then he noticed a small white cloud-like
object in an otherwise cloudless sky. He watched for about
five minutes as it traveled eastward; as it reached a spot north
northeast of his location, it abruptly altered shape from being
oblong and subtending about half the angle of the full moon
(about 15 minutes of arc) to being circular and subtending
about 5 minutes of arc. Webb was wearing polaroid glasses
and noted that there appeared around the object a series of
dark rings, the outermost of which was about six times the
diameter of the full moon. The object or cloud then decreased
in apparent diameter, as if it were traveling away from him,
and disappeared in another few minutes. During this time
Webb repeatedly took off his glasses and then put them back
on, noting each time that the rings appeared only when he was
wearing the glasses. He did not know what to make of the
sighting but took notes, including the fact that it was about 10
in the morning. The date: 5 May 1953.*

The next few paragraphs of the report then deal with the sighting
report in terms of the physics involved, which is somewhat com-
plicated and will not be dealt with here except to say that the report
indicates that the object must have had about it a very high magnetic field, in the range of over a million gausses, which accounts
for the rotation of the plane of polarization of the blue scattered
light that formed the background for the object. Yet to the naked
eye this object looked like a cloud! These observations can lead to
the conclusion that Jesus left this world in some type of magnetodynamic spaceship (Acts 1:9-10) and will return via the same
means at the head of a powerful space force (Mark 13:26; Rev.
1:7).

---

[3] Felix Zigel, "Unidentified Flying Objects," *Soviet Life,* Feb., 1968.

In conclusion, then, it can be stated that UFOs, present in earth's history since ancient times but more prevalent in the past twenty years, a period of time coincident with the reestablishment of Israel, are a real phenomenon. The phenomenological data, which is all remarkably alike in details, is being reported by reliable, sober, and in many instances highly competent persons from all over the world. The best hypothesis to explain the data is that the earth is under surveillance by vehicles whose technology-performance level is far above the limits of earth science and that the earth is the object of reconaissance by persons from an advanced extraterrestrial civilization. An examination of the relevant biblical data leads to the reasonable conclusion, when considering the present historical setting, that UFOs represent the space force of the Lord Jesus Christ preparing for the Second Coming. Some students of the UFO phenomenon have discovered by careful analysis that a pattern of increased UFO activity every five years can be discerned—1947, 1952, 1957, 1962, 1967. If this five-year pattern is projected forward, it will peak again in the year 1997, just prior to Israel's Year of Jubilee.

4 COMPUTERS, FOOD AND PEOPLE

The age of the computer is upon us, and no citizen of the world is unaware of that fact, especially as he files an income-tax return, which can be compared with other financial records with astonishing swiftness. Variations from the electronically coded data will bring tax men knocking on your door.

Rev. Billy Graham has correctly perceived in *World Aflame* that the appearance of computer technology will probably enable the Antichrist to control the life of every person on the face of the earth. In a manner similar to Hitler's Germany the world state will require a record of allegiance and worship of the world ruler. Those who fail to declare such allegiance and worship will be instantly detected by computer analysis and summarily dealt with. The conditions of George Orwell's *1984* will be more real than not. Each person now living in the United States now has a Social Security number which can be fed into a computer to detect quickly his location, place of employment, and income. Plans are even now being made to establish in this country a "National Data Bank," a concept which rightly frightens people because it is a portent of the future which lies almost immediately before mankind. With a "World Data Bank" it is easy to see how a powerful leader at the head of a one-world government could control the life and decide the very existence of every individual on the face of the earth. The wedding of the computer with a global telecommunications system would provide the mechanism for absolute control of the world's population. The question that arises in one's mind is, What global conditions could lead to such a political situation? There are indications appearing within contemporary history that just such conditions are brewing.

THE YEAR THE U.S. CAN'T FILL THE FOOD GAP

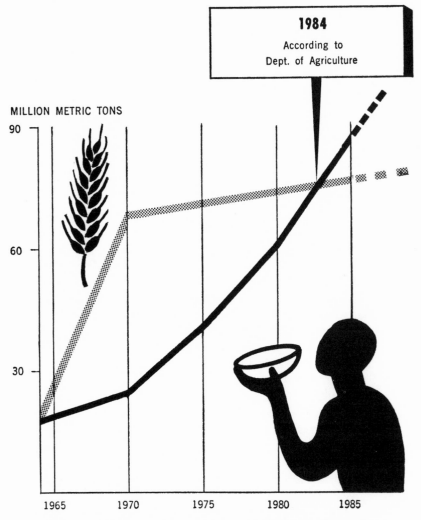

1984
According to
Dept. of Agriculture

MILLION METRIC TONS

Grain that could be produced in U.S. in excess of amounts needed for domestic use and commercial exports

Food aid needs of 66 developing countries

Many authors, such as William and Paul Paddock in their well-documented *Famine—1975,* are pointing out that the world population is rising at an astounding rate—in 1966 alone by some 70 million—without a compensatory improvement in food production. Various estimates have placed the coming world population by the year 2000 at between 5 and 7 billion. There are differing estimates also of when the critical point will be reached when America can no longer continue to feed other nations as she has done in the past. However, it appears that the critical point will be reached sometime between 1975 and 1985. When food resources are outstripped by the demand of the skyrocketing world population, governments will be forced to become more authoritarian as they seek to control the reproductive functions of their citizens. The 1980s will be the period of the regional famines which will probably be the precipitating motivation for the outbreak of World War III, which, as Arnold Toynbee has pointed out, is historically "overdue." One can expect that with the food crisis, governments will take vigorous, harsh steps to impose their will upon the populace they control, with a consequent loss of human freedoms. One of the most distressing of mankind's problems in food production, land erosion, has only recently become the focus of scientific attention and general concern. This problem is in many ways a moral one. If centuries ago the Spaniards had not cut most of their forests down to create vast naval fleets in pursuit of greedy imperial conquest, the resultant land erosion which has left Spain a relatively unfertile land would not have occurred.[1] In modern-day America these same pressures upon our timberlands need to be resisted so that our most vital treasure, our fertile soil in which to grow crops, will be preserved. Considered in a global context however, deforestation, ignorant soil management, and ecological ineptness have reduced, and are reducing, seriously the amount of arable soil upon which our food production depends. As the worldwide capacity to grow food drops the world population rises, thus eventually producing a catastrophic crisis. It will come in our lifetime.

---

[1] This reference should not be construed to view the Spaniards as being any more greedy than the rest of humanity. In the history of the world there is enough greediness to go around for everybody.

5 THE WORLD CHURCH

The concept of one Lord, one Faith, one Baptism, underlay the monolithic medieval Catholic Church. Man's propensity for idolatry, however, resulted in changing the simple New Testament era's church model into something hardly recognizable as a biblical institution. In the first century the church was characterized by true faith, missionary zeal, humility, and love. In these latter days the church organizations seem to be characterized by the size of their stockholdings, with some exceptions. In many denominational structures an idolatrous travesty of the community of disciples was and has been formulated as programs replaced the simple truth that Jesus taught as the way into His kingdom, namely, the necessity for the "new birth" via the working of the Holy Spirit in the soul of each individual person.

When Martin Luther appeared upon the scene, this monolithic structure was sharply split in the West. The earlier split with Byzantium had separated the Western and Eastern sections of the church. The Protestant Reformation, coupled with the rise of nationalism in Western Europe, paved the way for a diversification of expression of the Christian faith which resulted in some instances in a purer expression of the original will and intent of the Founder of the faith.

With the diversification of denominational expression there have been both advantages and disadvantages as purer, more realistic, biblically oriented, and efficient modes of expression of Christ's will have been formulated into various church organizations. At the same time, Christians have sometimes majored in minor matters and caused divisions among brethren over secondary and nonessential matters. One can speculate that the Lord Jesus may have some words of reproof for those who have artificially created divisions among His followers and of praise for those who have healed some of these ancient social wounds in the church without, of course, compromising essential principles. Infringement upon clear moral issues and the basic integrity of the Christian message cannot be tolerated as the price for an easy communion and accommodation among church organizations.

The ecumenical movement which has appeared upon the scene of world society within recent decades is a two-edged sword. On the one hand, it is beneficial that Christians who love the Lord Jesus are becoming more united in worship, fellowship, and evangelical concern and action. On the other hand, one can see in the growing ecumenical movement the beginning of the development of both administrative framework and mental attitude that can bring about the fulfillment of an ancient prophecy in Revelation regarding an end-time apostate world "church" (Rev. 17).

This chapter in Revelation has been interpreted by many to refer to an amalgamation of all religious groups and churches throughtout the world in the end-time, to include people of all faiths—Christian, Moslem, Hindu, Buddhist, and the others. These diverse groups may be unified around such vague and nondemanding slogans as "brotherhood," representing a lukewarm humanism, while the lordship of Jesus Christ is essentially ignored. Prophecy has been interpreted for many years to the effect that the world church organization would mistakenly assist the Antichrist in his initial efforts to mold the world into a global dictatorship. Indeed, there are suggestions in the prophecy that after the departure from this planet of the "true church" via the Rapture, the pseudo church will assist the Antichrist in his world rule. Some persons will, however, realize finally who he is and call upon the name of the Lord Jesus Christ for salvation during this most difficult and evil time of earth's history. When they do so, they will "come out" of the false and apostate church and suffer martyrdom as a concommitant of their act of faith in Christ.

That such a concentration of evil power motivated by greed, cruelty, and arrogance could characterize the alleged Christian church may be repugnant to the fair-minded 20th-century man, but the same attitudes which produced the horrors of the Roman circus and the St. Bartholomew's massacre still lurk in the hearts of men who are unconverted. During this period of seven years before the Second Coming, Satan will be permitted to have through the Antichrist full power over mankind and this planet. It may be that only thus can God in His wisdom demonstrate to the entire universe the true malignity of evil. The history of this planet would therefore be seen as having significance not only for earthpeople but for the citizens of other worlds as well.

Recent ecumenical developments confirm the prior prophetic stance of some theological interpreters of Revelation 17 to the effect that the great "whore" (the apostate end-time church) will sit upon the "beast" (the anti-christian world empire). An evil amalgamation of church and state! Rev. 17:15:

> *"And he said to me, 'The waters that you saw, where the harlot is seated, are peoples and multitudes and nations and tongues.'"*

If one considers carefully the phrasing of the recent Consultation on Church Union in reference to its "confession of Creed," it can be seen that the structuring of this aspect of church union is so nebulous that the new church will have an organization composed of people with irreconcilable and conflicting viewpoints! This ill-conceived alliance will eventually become a hindrance to Christian people wishing to unite on the basis of biblical truth. The result will be a vague kind of watered-down Christianity in which it will be felt that "it doesn't matter what you believe or do." God has outlined a different program for the true believer to approach Him through a Christ-committed life.

Ecumenism seems to be a blind spot in the eyes of some churchmen. It has not provided the spiritual stimulus expected of it. Those churches which are most prominent in the ecumenical movement and seeking to involve the church in more and more secular concerns are discovering that they have a faltering church on their hands. Their idol of clay is crumbling before their eyes. This failure may lead to renewed attempts to enlist the power of the state in "spiritual" endeavors. History teaches that clerical statism can produce the most vicious of political tyrannies.

The secret of the renewal of the church lies in each individual member's humbly connecting in a personal relationship with Jesus Christ as Lord and Saviour. But if church and state are combined in the new world empire by the Antichrist, then we shall see the apostate church, the "whore," sit upon the "beast," the civil power. The result will be a betrayal of the true gospel by religious leadership that is corrupt, false, and incompetent.

6 WORLD WAR III PROSPECTS

With the breaking out of armed clashes along the Russian-Chinese border in the early part of 1969 a new dimension was added to the international political situation. Many historians, among them Toynbee, have predicted that the time will come when the "Russian-Orthodox Empire" has to find shelter with the West against increasing pressure from the Sinic civilization.

Historically, contending power blocs have settled the issue of supremacy by a bout of force of arms. However, in the current weaponry situation, which has prevailed since World War II, restraint has been evidenced by world leaders, since the end result of such a bout could conceivably destroy a large portion of the human race and its civilization. A global situation has been produced without parallel in the history of the world. Even so, the frightening aspect of current history is that in the Cuban missile crisis of 1962 the world was ready to fight a nuclear war!

Intelligent voices in many lands have been raised to point out the deadly perils that mankind stands in today. Andrei D. Sakharov of the USSR, one of the world's most brilliant physicists, has made the following estimation:

The division of mankind threatens it with destruction. Civilization is imperiled by a universal thermonuclear war, catastrophic hunger for most of mankind, stupefaction from the narcotic of mass culture, and bureaucratized dogmatism, a spreading of mass myths that put entire peoples and continents under the power of cruel and treacherous demagogues, and destruction or degeneration from the unforeseeable consequences of swift changes in conditions of life on our planet.[1]

[1] *Progress, Coexistence and Intellectual Freedom* (New York, Norton, 1968), p. 27.

Many such voices have echoed throughout the world, most with despair and pessimism as they calculate the cost of the increasing armaments race among the nations of the world. The average citizen has little comprehension of the devastation that will occur if a thermonuclear-bacteriological war is unleashed upon the world. Probably 30 percent of the people of the world will perish. But even "beyond the bomb," other weapons are now being made ready in the arsenals of mankind. Nigel Calder, in his symposium *Unless Peace Comes,* has collected the observations of several international scientists who point out with terrifying clarity the potential global catastrophe. Toxic, bacteriological, and electromagnetic weapons are being devised to destroy mankind with increasing efficiency. In surveying the prospects for World War III the optimist is prone to come up with the old cliché that "war is so horrible it won't happen"—a point of view that history has consistently shown to be wrong. The pessimist sees the utter destruction of life in this world. The truth, as usual, would seem to lie somewhere between these two extremes.

All politicians are promising "peace and security," yet these are illusions in our world where evil reigns in the hearts of men. Arnold Toynbee was right when he described a "time of troubles" to continue through the latter third of this century. The rise of a monolithic China with nuclear-missile power is a hard fact of this century that most statesmen have yet to deal with realistically. The Middle East, a powder keg because it is the land-oceanic axis of the earth, can lead to a major confrontation of big powers at any time.

I have mentioned before the internal and external dangers to our national existence and freedoms. They were perceptively noted by Thomas B. Macaulay in 1857:

> *Either some Caesar or Napoleon will seize the reins of government with a strong hand, or your Republic will be as fearfully plundered and laid waste by barbarism in the 20th Century as the Roman Empire was in the 5th—with this difference—that your Huns and Vandals will be engendered within your own country by your own institutions.*

In man's current nationalistic searches for security America has

The city of Hiroshima smashed to rubble by one atomic bomb. More powerful bombs are now available, and during World War III many modern cities will end up like this.

made some mistakes which hopefully can be repaired. If not they will tempt some of the nations of the world to initiate World War III. There are various theoretical models of global and national security. They are (1) continental-based land power, (2) oceanic mobile power, and (3) aerospace strategy. The first model has been followed by America for years and because of our two oceans has been adequate. It no longer is; and it is ominous that the USSR has noted the significance of this and in recent years allocated considerable resources to building a naval force that will soon be the equal of America's. Indeed, there are some indications that their submarine forces are now superior to ours. The technological changes of earth science make an oceanic strategic power concept of greater use than the older continental land mass power.[2] It was probably his perception of this that led General MacArthur to caution against America's ever getting involved in a *land* war in Asia, since strategically it is a mistake. These constant errors of human thinking are continuing to occur, so that the Christian cannot expect "peace in our time"; but the words of our Lord, "wars and rumors of wars . . . but the end is not yet" (Matt. 24:6), will be an accurate historical guideline! To the Christian the cloying blandishments of the seductive Antichrist in regard to establishing world peace must be received with skepticism. The United Nations cannot at present be the answer to the ills of the world, since it is too fragmented and has no intrinsic power. The prime reason is that nationalism is still a very viable political system on our shrinking globe.

Under the pressure of population growth without a compensatory increase in food production governments of the world will begin to become desperate about 1980. The growth of friendlier relations between the United States and the Soviet Union will possibly eventuate in an alliance of sorts against the menacing power of the Chinese.[3] In the early 1980s World War III will probably break out with an attack by the Chinese and certain African na-

---

[2] For a fuller development of these problems see Hansen W. Baldwin, *Strategy for Tomorrow* (New York, Harper & Row, 1970).

[3] Harrison Salisbury, *War Between Russia and China* (New York, Norton, 1969), pp. 207-11.

tions against Russia and the West. Sophisticated bacteriological weapons will probably be used first, since it will be a primary aim in the war to be able to seize resources, not to destroy them, while at the same time eliminating people; however, the war will probably escalate to the use of more destructive weaponry rather rapidly. It may be at this time that Russia itself will seek to invade Israel from the north, and be destroyed as described by so many commentators on the basis of Ezekiel 38; or this may happen at a later date. The reader should not let slight differences of opinion over prophetic details cause him to lose sight of the prime purpose of this study, which is to clarify the point that the Second Coming of the Lord Jesus Christ is approaching in the foreseeable future and that only through Him is man saved.

The end result of World War III, which may be worse in some parts of the world than in others, will be a world populace desperate for peace. They will want to create some semblance of international order out of the atomic wreckage. From an ideological standpoint, nationalism will be dropped and replaced by internationalism. At this point, if a strong and brilliant leader appears who can transform the United Nations into a true federal world union with United Nations armed forces, the people of the earth will mistakenly think that a golden age has come instead of seeing the resultant world tyranny that will also come.

7 THE ANTICHRIST

For millenniums the Bible has foretold the rise of a world dictator who will be the personification of evil as Jesus was the personification of good. The connection in which the word Antichrist is used appears to import opposition, covert rather than avowed, with a professed friendliness.

The general view of Scripture is that this person will be satanically directed so that he will exhibit unusual powers of mind and be able to effect the structuring of a tightly controlled global social organization similar to that of Hitler's Germany. In this respect it is important to properly assess Hitler's position within the context of history. I lived in Germany for several years and had the opportunity to observe the physical and emotional scars the Hitlerian regime had inflicted upon not only mankind but also upon the German people.

In the historical experience of Nazi Germany one outstanding event commands the consideration of every thinking Christian. The Jews, God's Chosen People, were selected for deliberate annihilation. Anti-Semitism has long puzzled the rational observer of world history. The Jews are no better or worse in essence than the general lot of mankind (although figures show that they tend to be somewhat more law-abiding and responsible citizens than their gentile neighbors). What accounts, then, for the immense social hostility generated against them throughout history? The analyst who attempts to answer this question in merely human terms will not find satisfaction. Instead one must look beneath the surface of historical events to discern the gigantic cosmic conflict that has been going on between God and Satan. Satan cannot harm God, so he directs his hatred against God's Chosen People. Nora Levin in *The Holocaust* has pointed out the often unnoticed fact that the continued activity of the Nazi attempt to destroy the Jewish people in the closing days of World War II actually diverted resources that could have been used to wage the war more successfully for the Germans. So far as I have been able to ascertain, there was only one Jew who sensed the real reason for the cataclysm that struck the European Jewish community. That man, now dead, was Dr. L. Kurland, the camp historian at the Nazi death camp of Treblinka.

COURTESY YIVO INSTITUTE FOR JEWISH RESEARCH, NEW YORK

Innocent Jewish men, women, and childen being rounded up by German troops in the Warsaw ghetto for shipment to the death camp at Auschwitz, where they were exterminated. Christians face a similar fate during the reign of the Antichrist. Commenting on the prophecy of Revelation 13, which outlines the activity of the Antichrist, Cardinal Newman wrote, "This persecution will be worse than any persecution before it."

> *More than any other man in Treblinka, Kurland was a witness. . . . He also said, "God is not concerned about my death or that of any other single Jew, but He is concerned about our collective disappearance." He saw these events as the fulfillment of the divine will. For if God exists—and He did exist for Kurland—nothing can happen that He has not willed. But since God is not an arbitrary being all this had to have a meaning. The holocaust that God was bringing on His people could not be gratuitous. It must represent a terrible warning. It was on this point that Kurland's thinking differed from that of most religious Jews. Whereas the religious saw the extermination of the Jews as a warning to the Jews alone, Kurland thought that it was a warning to the world, that God was using His people to say something to the world. . . . He had become the camp historian and day by day he wrote the chronicle of the fulfillment of God's will so future generations could discern the hidden meaning.[1]*

While Kurland sensed the essential fact that God had allowed His firstborn, Israel, to be sacrificed to warn the world of some great impending evil, he did not understand its full prophetic significance, being a Jew. To understand this significance one must turn to the New Testament. Christian prophetic interpreters have long pointed out that in the end-time of earth's history God will allow Satan to have his way through the person of the Antichrist, who will attempt to arrogate and receive unto himself the worship and loyalty that only God and His Son, the Lord Jesus, can rightfully require and receive; and that during the reign of the Antichrist social conditions will be so tightly controlled that no one will be able to carry on any economic activity (buy or sell) (Rev. 13:17) who does not have the "mark" of the world dictator. This mark may be some kind of ID card which will indicate that the bearer has sworn an oath of allegiance and worship to the world dictator. (Former military personnel will remember clearly that they could not buy anything in a post exchange unless they had an ID card.)

Those who call upon the name of Jesus Christ during this period of time when the world dictator is in power will find themselves marked for extinction and extermination as were the Jews under

---

[1] Jean F. Steiner, *Treblinka* (New York, Signet Books, 1968).

Hitler. Those readers who find this thesis hard to believe should remember not only the clear word of prophecy in Revelation but also that the Jews in Europe did not believe the initial reports of the deliberate policy of extermination which filtered back to their communities from the death camps. It is a wise man who learns from other people's experience. Christians living in the time of the rule of the Antichrist should beware of attempts to ship them to "labor centers," "resettlement areas," and similar euphemisms for concentration camps. These are some of the same expressions that the Nazis used to lull the Jews into walking to their own deaths. Another trick was "serialization," by which is meant the process of issuing various types of "cards" for various categories of persons, old, young, workers, nonworkers, skilled, unskilled, etc. Each particular group thought that with its own distinctive card, it was safe, thus dividing all groups and preventing their united action to save themselves. This was both deliberate deception and self-delusion. In the end all groups went to the gas chambers. Many persons will of course be martyred during the time of the Antichrist (Rev. 6:9-11), but some may be forewarned and flee, to survive in wilderness areas.

The question arises in this period of earth's history since Israel was established, Is there any indication that the Antichrist has been born? I point the reader to the following remarkable events.

There has appeared in the United States a remarkable woman, Mrs. Jeane Dixon of Washington, D.C. Many readers have read that she predicted President John F. Kennedy's death, in addition to making other equally accurate predictions. In evaluating her unique experience, I, in company with many other people, have come to the conclusion that she does indeed have some special prophetic gift. Her Christian life and personality can be attested to by the following comments. That she has had great influence with world leaders and has never attempted to commercialize her gift attests further to its validity. A few opinions about Mrs. Dixon follow.[2]

---

[2] Ruth Montgomery, *A Gift of Prophecy: The Phenomenal Jeane Dixon* (New York, Bantam Books, 1965), pp. 136, 140, 165.

*But A False Prophet Like
The Woman In Acts 16:16-18

I consider Mrs. Dixon to be an extraordinarily saintly person. In my investigations of her remarkable talents, she has no living peer.—F. REGIS RIESENMAN, M.D., *Psychiatrist, Washington, D.C.*

She is extremely devout. She is outgoing and kind, very definitely generous, and desirous of helping others. There is

COURTESY YIVO INSTITUTE FOR JEWISH RESEARCH, NEW YORK

A pile of starved, emaciated Jewish children killed at Auschwitz. The death of these innocents is a warning to the world of what will happen during the reign of the antichrist world dictator to Christians who will not worship him. To those people to whom the brutalities and deaths of the Nazi regime, including shoving naked men, women, children, and babies into gas chambers after degrading them in unspeakable ways, has seemed "impossible," this picture will be worth a thousand words. It is what the Tribulation saints can expect under the reign of the Antichrist (Rev. 6:9-11). The extermination process will be generated in part by the failing food supply of the planet Earth.

*not a drop of selfishness in her. She is a superior person in
every way.*—MSGR. JAMES A. MAGNER, *Catholic University
of America.*

    *She is a most interesting person! . . . very open in her at-
titude toward Christianity everywhere. She is a very magnan-
imous lady.*—REV. M. JOLLAY, *Pastor, Full Gospel Church,
Washington, D.C.*

It can be noted that Mrs. Dixon has been wrong on occasion.
Her visions seem to be of two varieties: (1) a clear revelation of
God's will, which comes to her unsought, as to what shall come
to pass, and (2) a cognition of certain human events which can
be altered by human choice and action. Mrs. Dixon has made the
following important observations about herself: "My symbols are
never wrong, but sometimes I misinterpret them." The visionary
experience of Mrs. Dixon that I would like to direct the attention
of the reader to is the one that she describes as the most important
of her life and that happened on February 5, 1962:

    *. . . she saw, not the barelimbed trees and city street below,
but a bright blue sky above a barren desert. Just above the
horizon was the brightest sun that she had ever seen, glowing
like a golden ball. Splashing from the orb in every direction
were brilliant rays which seemed to be drawing the earth
toward it like a magnet. Stepping out of the brightness of the
sun's rays, hand in hand, were a Pharaoh and Queen Nefertiti. Cradled in the Queen's other arm was a baby, his ragged,
soiled clothing in startling contrast to the gorgeously arrayed
royal couple. The eyes of this child were all-knowing, Jeane
says softly. They were full of wisdom and knowledge. A little
to one side of Queen Nefertiti, Jeane could glimpse a pyramid.
While she watched entranced the couple advanced toward her
and thrust forth the baby, as if offering it to the entire world.
Within the ball of the sun, Jeane saw Joseph guiding the tab-
leau like a puppeteer pulling strings. Now rays of light burst
forth from the baby, blending with those of the sun and
obliterating the Pharaoh from her sight. Off to the left, she
observed that Queen Nefertiti was walking away, "thousands
of miles into the past." The Queen paused beside a large
brown water jug, and as she stooped and cupped her hands to
drink she was stabbed in the back by a dagger. Jeane says that
she distinctly heard her death scream as she vanished. Jeane
shifted her gaze back to the baby. He had by now grown to*

*manhood, and a small cross which formed above him began
to expand until it dripped over the earth in all directions.
Simultaneously peoples of every race, religion, and color
(black, yellow, red, brown and white), each kneeling and lifting
his arms in worshipful adoration, surrounded him. They were
as one.*[3]

We now come to Mrs. Dixon's interpretation of her vision and
note by her own admission that she does not clearly understand
the significance of this vision in its completeness:

*A child born somewhere in the Middle East shortly after
7 A.M. on February 5, 1962, will revolutionize the world.
Before the close of the century he will bring together all
mankind in one all-embracing faith. This will be the founda-
tion of a new Christianity, with every sect and creed united
through this man who will walk among the people to spread
the wisdom of the Almighty Power. This person, though born
of humble peasant origin, is a descendant of Queen Nefertiti
and her Pharaoh husband; of this I am sure. There was nothing kingly about his coming—no kings or shepherds to do
homage to this newborn baby—but he is the answer to the
prayers of a troubled world. Mankind will begin to feel the
great force of this man in the early 1980s and during the
subsequent ten years the world as we know it will be re-
shaped and revamped into one without wars or suffering. His
power will grow greatly until 1999, at which time the peoples
of the earth will probably discover the full meaning of the
vision.*[4]

Some aspects of her vision, Mrs. Dixon failed to comment upon,
and they deserve mention. "Joseph" may be a symbolic reference
to the skill of this world leader in resolving the food/population
crisis when famines begin to break out in various parts of the
world in the 1980s. The experience of Joseph in the Old Testament in saving the land of Egypt from seven years of famine may
have been planned with some extremely long-range goals in mind
by God as a "type" of the future famine in the end-time. Another
aspect of the vision that is not commented upon is the malignant

---

[3] *Ibid.,* pp. 178-81.
[4] *Ibid.*

omen in the death by stabbing of the mother of this world leader. This in marked contrast to the mother of Jesus, who in her joy said, "For behold, henceforth all generations will call me blessed" (Luke 1:48).

When the time period of Mrs. Dixon's vision is examined, we note that she has outlined a period of activity for this world leader of exactly 37 years, no more, no less: February 5, 1962-1999. The student of biblical prophecy will find this period most intriguing, since one of the conceptions about the Antichrist is that he will seek to imitate Christ. Since Jesus began his public ministry at the age of 30 years (Luke 3:23), the Antichrist will seek to do the same. When 30 years are deducted from the above time segment, it can be seen that exactly 7 years are left—a period of time that has long been interpreted to be the duration of the reign of the Antichrist (Dan. 9:27) Here, then, finally arrived upon the scene of world history, is the long-predicted man of sin (II Thess. 2:1-12); (Rev. 13).

God is probably allowing Satan to have his will for a period of time through the Antichrist to demonstrate to the inhabitants of other worlds the true horrendous effects of evil when it has complete control over the inhabitants of an entire planet.

That this is the reason why God allows evil and has allowed it to exist for thousands of years is not really understood by many people. If God directly prevented evil from happening, man would no longer have a degree of authentic choice, which is his crowning glory in terms of an interpersonal relationship with his Creator. God has a higher interest in view, and so He sent his Son to demonstrate for all eternity His profound love for His created beings throughout the universe. In allowing the Antichrist to have his day in earth's history, God will be settling existentially an important cosmic issue. Bearing this fact in mind, the individual follower of God can see his personal difficulties in this world with more perspective and insight.

Since the world leader born in 1962 is of Egyptian origin, one might expect him to emerge upon the scene of world power as the leader of a pan-Arabic federation of some sort in the 1980s, when he reaches maturity; and it can be remembered that Egypt

became a province of the Roman Empire in 30 B.C. The reference
to "Pharaoh" may be understood if one conceptualizes the Pharaoh
in the Old Testament as a "type" of the Antichrist and his downfall in the Red Sea as a prefigurement of the downfall of the Antichrist in the Battle of Armageddon at the close of the period of the
Great Tribulation when the armies of all the earth are arrayed
against Israel. It can also be recognized that a "new Christianity"
would be a contradiction in terms and a complete impossibility.
In her new book *Jeane Dixon: My Life and Prophecies*, published
in 1969, Mrs. Dixon clarifies and elaborates on her 1962 vision,
clearly identifying the world leader born then as the long-expected
Antichrist who with a false prophet will deceive many people,
leading them into an idolatrous humanism that will in the end
destroy them. The multitudes of earth, except for a minority faithful to God and the Lord Jesus Christ, will forget the words from
Sinai: "You shall have no other gods before me." Mrs. Dixon bears
positive testimony to Jesus Christ as Lord, God, and Saviour.

Since some erroneous comments have appeared in print regarding Mrs. Dixon's prophetic role, it seems prudent to quote the
lady directly. She has written in regard to Jesus Christ as follows:[5]

> *Christ's message at birth was that of a loving Saviour who
> had come into the world to release His tortured creation from
> the bonds of Satan.*
>
> *Christ our Lord was the Divine Word made flesh, dwelling
> within us on this earth in the flesh. Therefore we Christians
> speak of His "Incarnation" and say that Jesus Christ is God
> Incarnate (in the flesh).*
>
> *Thus the doctrine of the Second Coming of Christ becomes
> an absolute truth in the Christian faith.*

In regard to the world leader she has seen born in 1962 in the
month of February, she has written as follows:

---

[5] Jeane Dixon, *Jeane Dixon: My Life and Prophecies* (New York,
Morrow, 1969), pp. 172, 187-88, 211. It should be noted that the conception of and belief in the Antichrist after Israel's rise again as a nation
is not original with Mrs. Dixon; it was the teaching of the N.T. writers
and the early church Fathers. The only *fact* that she supplies is the date
of his birth, in 1962. That he would appear in the last third of the 20th
century has been and is being expected by many biblical interpreters.

> *The circumstances surrounding the birth of the "Child of the East" and the events I have seen taking place in his life make him appear so Christlike, yet so different, that there is* <u>*no doubt in my mind that the "child" is the actual person of*</u> <u>*the Antichrist, the one who will deceive the world in Satan's*</u> <u>*name."*</u> *[Underscored lines italicized in Mrs. Dixon's book.]*[6]

While I have suggested that the Antichrist world dictator will arise initially as the leader of a pan-Arabic federation, an alternative hypothesis has been suggested that he will be the leader of an amalgamation of the nations of Western civilization, who will ultimately, however, become the world-empire dictator, since the prophecy of Rev. 13:7 states that the Antichrist will have worldwide authority: "And authority was given it over every tribe and people and tongue and nation. . . ."

---

[6] *Ibid.*

8 THE RAPTURE QUESTION

One aspect of the end-time events and the Second Coming that is not quite clear is that of the "Rapture." This is a topic that honest theologians have had some disagreements about, since the point of the Rapture in relationship to the period of the Great Tribulation is never clearly fixed in the Bible. An excellent study of this problem has been made by Rev. John P. Walvoord of Dallas Theological Seminary. In brief, however, it can be stated that the Rapture means "caught up," as mentioned in I Thess. 4:17, and that it refers to the removal of the true church of Christ, those "born-again" believers who are truly His followers from this planet. They are to be distinguished from those church members who are merely nominal and from the unchurched. The first half of the seven-year reign of the Antichrist is thought by some commentators to be a peaceful one; in the latter half the Great Tribulation will happen. Since the points of Rapture and Tribulation are not sharply dovetailed in Scripture, various opinions have emerged.

That the Rapture will be post-tribulational has been the majority view of the church and the traditional one. In brief it states that the Rapture, consisting of the first Resurrection and the translation of the living righteous, will happen shortly before or coincidental with the Second Coming. The church composed of all true believers will suffer severe persecution and endure the wrath of men under the Antichrist (Matt. 24:21). There are good Christian men who have seen these events differently. Those who see the post-tribulational position as correct—and this list is not complete—include Rev. Charles Spurgeon, Rev. Harold Ockenga, and Dr. Oswald J. Smith of Peoples Church, Toronto.

The mid-tribulational position is a minor view to the effect that the church will be raptured in the middle of the seven-year period and will be saved only from the last three and one-half years of the Tribulation.

A consideration of the Rapture doctrine brings into question the idea of "imminency," held by some modern-day Christians. This idea is really a development of theological views of the last century and a half. In my view it is unscriptural and misleading in that it lacks the integration and historical perspective of prophecy's unfolding scheme. It is not in accordance with Acts 3:20-21:

> ". . . the Christ, appointed for you, Jesus, whom heaven must receive until the time for establishing all that God spoke by the mouth of his holy prophets from of old."

The post-tribulational view of the Rapture will prepare Christians for the future. If it is the true view, they will need (1) faith to endure based on knowledge, conviction and commitment to God, (2) a piercing skepticism of the false wonders that the false prophet will show the populace of the earth, realizing that in the end he is backing a loser, (3) a zeal to witness for Christ and to face death if need be, relying on the promise of the Resurrection.

The post-tribulational view is admittedly a theological spare tire, but it behooves a prudent person to prepare for a contingency!

The imminent view of the Second Coming contradicts the plain teaching of II Thess. 2:1-3:

> "Now concerning the coming of our Lord Jesus Christ and our assembling to meet him, we beg you, brethren, not to be quickly shaken in mind or excited, either by spirit or by word, or by letter purporting to be from us, to the effect that the day of the Lord has come. Let no one deceive you in any way; for that day will not come, unless the rebellion comes first, and the man of lawlessness is revealed, the son of perdition, who opposes and exalts himself against every so-called god or object of worship, so that he takes his seat in the temple of God, proclaiming himself to be God."

The imminent view also contradicts Jesus' own words in Luke 21:28 and Mark 13:24-27.

When the Rapture does occur, if it is pre-tribulational one would not expect the Antichrist to suddenly jump out of the international woodwork!

He probably would have been detectable as a personage before the Rapture event but in low profile in comparison to his later supreme power in the world.

Knowledgeable biblical students will recognize him for who he really is, the tool of Satan.

The predominant view held today is that the church will be raptured before the seven-year Tribulation period begins. This view is based on the idea that the church is to be spared God's wrath (Rom. 5:9). In view of the fact that the Tribulation period is a pouring out of God's wrath (Rev. 6:17), the Rapture must remove the true church before this happens. This principle is shown in Gen. 19:22, where the angels could not begin to destroy Sodom until Lot and his family had been safely removed from the area.

Which view is correct? It is possible that both are, in that a pre-tribulational rapture could remove the true church; however, a new "true" church would begin to formulate and become the saints of the Tribulational period, and these new Christians would suffer death for their allegiance to God and His Christ. In a sense, then, this new church group, somewhat of a remnant church, will go through the Tribulation. These martyred people will be resurrected as the "gleanings" shortly before the actual Second Coming (Rev. 6:9-11; 7:13-14). In any case Christian teachers and pastors have to labor in the vineyard of the Lord to prepare *both* groups for salvation, and this viewpoint should be kept in mind as the gospel is preached. Among those not taken in the Rapture will be many who find Christ as Saviour and Lord and preach the gospel during the time the Antichrist rules over the earth.

The basic text for this belief of Christians is found in I Thess. 4: 16-18:

> *"For the Lord himself will descend from heaven with a cry*
> *of command, with the archangel's call and with the sound of*
> *the trumpet of God. And the dead in Christ will rise first: then*
> *we who are alive, who are left, shall be caught up together*

with them in the clouds to meet the Lord in the air; and so we shall always be with the Lord."

An elucidation of the meaning of these "clouds" may be taken from the fact that Jesus left this planet in a "cloud" (Acts 1:9) and stated definitely that He would return with great power in a "cloud" (Mark 13:6; Luke 21:27; Rev. 1:7). In years gone by some artists have portrayed Him returning to earth seated on a real cloud, a somewhat unsubstantial type of vehicle for space travel. As developed in a prior chapter, the real meaning of the "cloud" must relate to some type of highly technically advanced magnetodynamic spaceship.

Since we shall be caught up "in clouds," as the original Greek reads, this connotes a vast and highly organized space fleet to remove the redeemed from this planet. The exact details of this event are not fully clarified in Scripture.

The question whether or not the church must go through the Great Tribulation has, as noted, led to disagreement among equally pious and learned men (Matt. 24:15-22). Since the church "ecclesia" are not appointed to God's wrath but are saved from it by Christ's atoning sacrifice, it would appear sensible that they do not suffer through the Tribulation, which consists of God's judgments upon an unrepentant world. These judgments are described in some detail in the early chapters of the book of Revelation and are referred to later in this study. They will create unimaginable ecological upheavals upon the planet Earth.

In I Cor. 15:51-52 we read:

"Lo! I tell you a mystery. We shall not all sleep, but we shall all be changed, in a moment, in the twinkling of an eye, at the last trumpet. For the trumpet will sound, and the dead will be raised imperishable, and we shall be changed."

The translation of the living redeemed at the time of the Rapture and First Resurrection implies some modification of man's current body structure into a state of perfection and youthful vitality. If this process were to immediately precede the Second Coming, when Christ returns to found His Messianic kingdom and rule over the earth, then His promise that *"where I am you may be also*" would seem to be pointless. Therefore the Rapture event must precede in some time the actual Second Coming, which we know is after the start of the reign of the Antichrist and the subsequent Great Tribulation.

As to the location of the "where" of Jesus' words in John 14: 1-3, one can easily imagine in earth's Space Age an answer to that question. In most discussions of the Rapture event little attention is paid to the question, *Where* are we going? The astronomers in the modern age can help us with this question. Not only from the field of empirical thinking but also from the science of astronomy have come evidences that there are many other suns in the multitude of galaxies in the universe that are similar to our own sun. If only a small percentage of these suns have planets similar to earth rotating in space around them, this percentage would provide millions of inhabitable planets—truly "many abiding places" in our Father's house, the universe.

On many of these earthlike planets the Lord Jesus Christ has caused to be prepared for His people from earth shining cities, homes, gardens, and work areas. These worlds now lie silent except for caretakers' footsteps. During the sojourn of earth-people on these worlds they will appear before Christ's judgment seat for a determination of rewards to be given as a result of works done to advance the cause of the kingdom of God during their lifetimes. The Rapture event therefore concerns only the saved, while the Second Coming deals with the saved and the unsaved.

The translation of the church coupled with the First Resurrection is pictured as a deliverance before the day of wrath, while the Second Coming is followed by the deliverance of those who have believed in Christ during the Tribulation, both Jew and Gentile.

The most important point about the Rapture is to be ready for it spiritually and morally. Such readiness is attained by a vital, continuing relationship with God by daily consecration, prayer, and Bible study. By doing so one can walk humbly before God and "abide" in Christ.

9 JESUS THE CHRIST AND HIS KINGDOM

"In the beginning God created the heavens and the earth." These majestic words spoken from space at Christmas time, 1968, develop the problem of the origin of the universe, our own world, and mankind.

Did Adamic man begin to exist in a moment of time as implied by Genesis, or did he evolve from slime on some primeval seashore? The evolutionist exhibiting his own great faith has the problem of explaining the seashore to begin with. From where and how did matter itself come? If we did not see the redemptive footprints of God throughout history, we would be forced to see Him as the Great Intelligence who alone can account for the "integral of all the only intellectually conceivable weightless, generalized principles discovered by science to be omni-operative as governing every physical" change.[1]

To understand the story of the Christ-Person, one must consider some aspects of man's behavior. The Bible, a hardy survivor of civilization's disasters, bears considerable internal, historical and archeological evidence of its basic validity. Some of the problems associated with understanding its message are related to the fact that original manuscripts are not available and sometimes the record is incomplete (John 20:30; 21:25). This situation has created certain minor intellectual problems in dealing with and evaluating the biblical documents, since textual variations have occurred in the transmission-copying process, although less so in the Old Testament. However, when these are all examined they become problems of minutiae, not of substance.

---

[1] Buckminster Fuller, "Man with a Chronofile," *Saturday Review,* Apr. 1, 1967.

The important and considerable fact which emerges is that the Bible does constitute a reliable communication of God's will and love for mankind. It has stood the test of time and in both general and specific items been validated by history, archeology, and human experience as a source to which man can turn for understanding and hope.

From the far-flung vast "island universe" galaxies to the symmetrical, minute perfection of the atomic particles of matter, nature points to a Designer on a grand and infinite scale.

How can God be one, yet three? is a question theologians have puzzled over for millenniums.[2] The answer may lie in our attempting to construct God in our own image and on the level of our own physical comprehension. But man is, in his present state of physical existence, matter-bound. If God's "form-structure" is able to oscillate freely between matter and energy, some variations in theophanies become obvious.

The size of the universe and its vast distances stagger the imagination, what with our galaxy, one of millions, being itself some 100,000 light-years in diameter. Ancient man had no conception of the universe in which he lived; he saw only a handful of the stars that truly exist.

In dealing with the creation of man—the original pair, Adam and Eve—recent biological discoveries enable us to comprehend with much more exactitude that man is truly "intricately wrought" (Ps. 139:15). The discovery of the DNA code system by Nobel Prize winners Crick, Watson, and Wilkins has revealed to us that the basic "life stuff" of the chromosomes we received from our parents and pass on to our children is an intricate double-coiled coded tape which "orders" the development of a new individual with all the exquisite, anatomical, physiological and molecular-atomic design structure when sperm meets egg in the act of love. In this double helix are molecularly configured billions of "bits of information" as to the details of each new person, down to blueprints for the chemical reactions inside various types of cells. Yet when we look further at the atomic structure of the molecules

---

[2] The Hebrew word for God, *Elohim,* is plural.

composing the body structure, we realize that matter being congealed energy, as it were, is an expression of an electromagnetic force field in a certain pattern mold. Recent studies have also shown that there exists universally about each person's body a biomagnetic field which disappears at death. The "soul," therefore, may be some kind of electromagnetic energy template which snaps free from the body as we know it at the point of death and is available to be used by God in the resurrection process.

Certainly the earth is an ancient piece of equipment, as attested to by geological evidences, but it is reasonable to conclude that Adamic man was created about 25000-15000 B.C., with subsequent generations perishing in the flood of Noah, which some geological evidence dates at about 9000 B.C. Recent archeological evidence points to the Anatolian plateau as the site of the first agricultural villages (7000 B.C.) rather than the Mesopotamian valley—a correlative confirmation of Gen. 11:2. Subsequently, with the rise of Sumer, the call to Abraham was made. An examination of the historical records of ancient Sumeria reveals man to be the same then as now—prone to greed, lust, killing, and all the other evil practices so prevalent in the 20th century.

The idea of "original sin" seems an unpopular one in this day and age, but I have concluded after an examination of various psychobiological-theory constructs to explain human behavior that the biblical model has the most going for it. It is therefore completely relevant if one is to intelligently understand the world we live in. Secondarily there are various neurological and psychiatric disturbances that afflict mankind, but before these can be considered there seems to be a problem of a primary behavioral disturbance. I have concluded that the idea of a primary behavioral bent seems to best answer the need for a theoretical model that will explain mankind's inept handling of himself throughout history and in various cultures.

Did the eating of the tree of good and evil actually trip some electromagnetic structure in the DNA code? Or is this only a poetic story of the act of disobedience toward God?

It is interesting to note that physiologists are becoming more convinced that man should not die, since the body cells, with the notable exception of nerve cells, are constantly replenishing themselves. It would appear that, barring disease or accident, this could continue indefinitely; but because of some subtle influence the replacement process is imperfect. The fruit of the tree of life may have been an enzymatic substance that would clear the genetic DNA code on a cellular level and also allow nerve cells to replenish as other cells do. This arrangement would have kept man from aging and also at the same time reminded man that he was a mortal being dependent on God for his existence.

Who was this man, Jesus of Nazareth? This question has been debated as no other for centuries by learned men. Was He truly more than mere man? Was He God incarnate in human form? Such a conception, while at first incredible, becomes after an examination of the issues involved quite a reasonable conclusion. In conceptualizing the doctrine of the Christ-Person it can be understood more readily if one imagines oneself viewing this world's historical process from another planet, perhaps via transgalactic television.

Basically the teaching of the Bible in its greater scope is that man broke the polarity-love relationship with God. This, more than any specific act, is what "sin" amounts to. Sin, therefore, can be understood as a persistent tendency within man's psychobiological nature toward what Will Herberg calls "self-absolutization" —an existential term of great usefulness. The term portrays perhaps more than mere selfishness the appalling and self-destructive tendency of mankind to focus and internalize psychic energy upon the self rather than turning it outward toward God and fellow humans so that a socially orderly and constructive society can be built.

One can see that God was faced with the problem of evil when the original parents broke their love relationship with Him. If man were to achieve in his present state of mind nuclear weapons and the ability to travel throughout the universe, he could destroy the whole transgalactic civilization. Other peaceful worlds could and would be looted if earthmen wanted their resources.

In viewing mankind's predicament, within the great heart of God the Son the purposeful love in action formulated the plan of

A unique painting of the Crucifixion by Salvador
Dali depicting the trans-historical and omni-temporal
meaning of the sacrifice of Christ for mankind.
Amidst the troubled events of the next thirty years
the Christian can rest in the promise that "I am
sure that neither death . . . nor principalities . . .
nor powers, nor anything else in all creation, will
be able to separate us from the love of God in
Christ Jesus our Lord" (Rom. 8:38-39).

salvation so that man through Christ could have a second chance to achieve his divine heritage. To willingly incarnate Himself into humanity so that He might suffer the death of the Cross and thus balance the scales of divine justice for us bespeaks a magnificent quality of cosmic love. The God-Man had to come of the line of the people chosen for a special communication between God and mankind, namely, the Jewish people, who were formulated as the mystery of Israel. A careful examination of the whole point of the experience of Israel reveals that the claims of Jesus of Nazareth rest upon one cardinal point! Was He the Messiah of Israel or not? Some of the prophecies that He fulfilled are as follows: (1) Born of the seed of Abraham (Gen. 49:10; Heb. 7:14). (2) Of the lineage of David (II Sam. 7:16; Rom. 1:3). (3) His birthplace in Bethlehem (Mic. 5:2; Matt. 2:1-6). (4) To enter Jerusalem on an ass (Zech. 9:9; Matt. 21:4-5). (5) To be buried with the rich (Isa. 53:9; Matt. 27:57-60). The whole point of Isaiah 53 is that the suffering servant shall be an offering for the sins of mankind and that later He shall see the fruitage of the travail of His soul, the redeemed persons of earth, and be satisfied. Through the sacrifice on Calvary, Christ fulfilled the plan of Isaiah 53 and died for the sins of mankind, thus opening the way for salvation to all who will call upon His name and accept Him as Saviour and Lord. The implication of the resurrection of Christ is stated in Isa. 53:11. Jesus upon the Cross experienced the anguish of the sinner's separation from God.

In the councils of the transgalactic civilization—the "kingdom of heaven"—the news of mankind's disobedience must have produced considerable discussion. God apparently had three choices: (1) Destroy the original pair. (2) Allow mankind to live, procreate and eventually blow the planet Earth apart all by themselves—an event some people are working toward at the present time. (3) Set into effect a complex judicial, trans-historical, communicative, redemptive plan to give mankind a second chance and deal with the question of evil fully and with finality. If He had not done so, the tears of the children of earth would have echoed unanswered throughout the universe. This complex plan had to be accomplished by the "new Adam," winning back the sovereignty of the

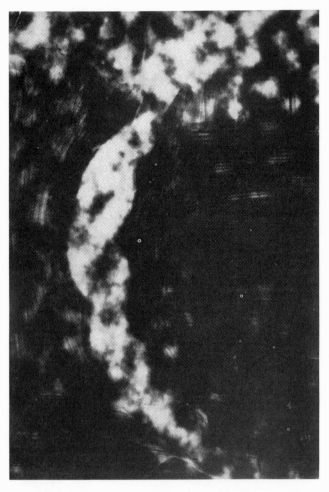

An actual photograph, magnified some seven million times by the electron microscope, reveals the DNA helix in all its wondrous intricacy (Ps. 139:15). This little loop of the basic genetic material is a coiled, coded, molecular tape which orders the construction of a new individual with billions of working parts.

earth. It was not only to pay the judicial penalty that humanity deserved but also to win for them the right to eternal life by loving obedience to God that Jesus voluntarily went to the hill of Calvary (Luke 9:30-31).

The Bible clearly implies in Mic. 5:2 and Isa. 9:6-7 that the Christ-Person will be God incarnate, and so Jesus claimed to be (Ex. 3:14; John 8:56-58). The mystery of how this was done is indeed complex genetically. However, in reading Phil. 2:5-7, if one can visualize this "form" of God as a life-form structure that can oscillate between matter and energy freely, then the Incarnation can be understood on a scientific level perhaps somewhat more clearly. Studies of memory mechanisms have shown that this must exist on a molecular level within the some 13 billion brain cells. If the preexistent memory-constructs of God the Son were programmed within an electromagnetic field to couple with the DNA in Mary, then the Incarnation can be understood as a rational though awesome process and can explain many of Christ's comments regarding His pre-earthly existence (John 6:38). My theoretical formulation can be suggestive only; some aspects of Jesus' divine sonship defy human comprehension. Scripture implies that God the Son surrendered some of the prerogatives of deity (I Cor. 15:24; Phil. 2:6-7) in order to effect our salvation. This should not cause us to respect Him any less, but to love Him more, because of the great love He demonstrated for us. That Jesus actually lived on earth is not disputed by responsible scholars. His birth was heralded as He was born King of the Jews (Matt. 2:1-2; Luke 2:25-32); and old Simeon saw Him as the light of the world.

The mathematical improbability that Jesus of Nazareth could fulfill so many prophetic details of His Messianic role and yet not be the long-awaited Saviour assumes unbelievable proportions. It is obvious that Jesus had to fulfill many items biographically in order to be recognized clearly as the Messiah. Prophecy is His pre-written role, which must be congruent with biography.

PROPHECY	Equals	BIOGRAPHY
Gen. 3:15	*seed of a woman*	*Gal. 4:4; Luke 2:7; Rev. 12:5*
Gen. 18:18	*seed of Abraham*	*Acts 3:25;*
Gen. 12:3		*Matt. 1:1; Luke 3:34*
Gen. 17:19	*seed of Isaac*	*Matt. 1:2; Luke 3:34*
Num. 24:17	*seed of Jacob*	*Luke 3:34; Matt. 1:2*
Gen. 49:10	*The tribe of Judah*	*Luke 3:33; Matt. 1:2-3*
Isa. 9:7		
Isa. 11:1-5	*The throne of David*	*Matt. 1:1,6*
II Sam. 7:13		
Mic. 5:2	*place of birth*	*Matt. 2:1; Luke 2:4-7*
Dan. 9:25	*time of birth*	*Luke 2:1-7*
Isa. 7:14	*born of a virgin*	*Matt. 1:18; Luke 1:26-35*
Jer. 31:15	*slaughter of the infants*	*Matt. 2:16-18*
Hos. 11:1	*flight into Egypt*	*Matt. 2:14-15*
Isa. 9:1-2	*ministry in Galilee*	*Matt. 4:12-16*
Deut. 18:15	*prophetic mission*	*John 1:45; 6:14; Acts 3:19-26*
Ps. 110:4	*a priest of the order of Melchizedek*	*Heb. 5:5-6; 6:20; 7:15-17*
Isa. 53:3	*rejection by his own people*	*John 1:11; John 5:43 Luke 4:17-25, 29; 23:18*
Zech. 9:9	*triumphal entry into Jersusalem*	*John 12:12-14; Matt. 21:1-11*
Isa. 62:11		
Ps. 41:9	*Betrayed by a friend*	*Mark 14:10, 43-45; Matt. 26:14-16*
Zech. 11:12-13	*thirty pieces of silver*	*Matt. 26:15; 27:3-10*
Ps. 27:12	*the victim of false witnesses*	*Matt. 26:60-61*
Ps. 35:11		
Isa. 53:7	*silent before accusers*	*Matt. 26:62:63; 27:12-14*
Ps. 38:13-14		
Isa. 50:6	*smitten and spat upon*	*Mark 14:65; 15:17; John 18:22; 19:1-3*
Ps. 69:4	*hated without a cause*	*John 15:23-25*
Ps. 109:3-5		
Isa. 53:4-12	*suffered*	*Matt. 8:16-17; Rom. 4:25; I Cor. 15:3*

Isa. 53:12	*crucified*	*Matt. 27:38; Luke 23:33; Mark 15:27-28*
Ps. 22:16 *Zech. 12:10*	*pierced*	*John 19:34-37; 20:25-27*
Ps. 22:6-8	*mocked*	*Matt. 27:39-44; Mark 15:29-32*
Ps. 69:21	*given gall and vinegar to drink*	*John 19:29; Matt. 27:34-48*
Ps. 22:18	*soldiers cast lots*	*Mark 15:24; John 19:24*
Ex. 12:46 *Ps. 34:20*	*not a bone broken*	*John 19:33*
Isa. 53:9	*buried with the rich*	*Matt. 27:57-60*
Ps. 16:10	*the resurrection*	*Matt. 28:9; Luke 24:36-48[3]*

It becomes apparent in studying biblical prophecies that God uses two general methods. One is that future events are revealed in bits and pieces, not as a comprehensive whole; and the other is that such revelation of future events is a progressive one. We in the modern era are able to understand many conceptions of prophecy that our ancestors could only wonder about. There are many unfulfilled prophecies of Christ that await completion at the time of the Second Coming and during the Millennial Kingdom. A partial list is here given to help outline the future.

He shall return as he ascended	*Acts 1:11*
He shall stand on the Mount of Olives	*Zech 14:4*
Every eye shall see him	*Rev. 1:7*
The dead shall rise in the resurrection	*I Cor. 14:52*
The living shall be given immortality	*I Thess. 4:17*
The redeemed shall meet him in the air	*I Thess. 4:17*
He shall judge the works of the redeemed	*II Cor. 5:10*

---

[3] Robert Witty, *Signs of the Second Coming* (Nashville, Tenn., Broadman Press, 1969), pp. 43-47. Used by permission.

He shall reward his redeemed for their works	Rev. 22:12
He shall destroy the Antichrist	II Thess. 2:8
He shall ascend the throne of David	Matt. 25:31; Isa. 9:6-7
He shall rule over the whole earth	Rev. 11:15; I Cor. 6:2
His apostles shall reign over Israel	Luke 22:28-30
Peace shall be universal	Mic. 4:3[4]

Jesus came to effect a deep revolution within men, to cleanse the heart of lust, selfishness, and aggressive cruelty. In this sense Christ was a far greater revolutionist than Karl Marx. His ideas were not different from the teachings of the Old Testament prophets, but their arrangement was. He came to effect the plan of salvation, validating it by His death, and to select a group of men to carry on His work after He had left earth. At first glance they were a mixed crew—friendly John; impulsive, cowardly Peter; honest-hearted Nathanael; the "sons of thunder," who included James; a hated tax collector, Matthew; and the scientist Thomas. A most diverse group, yet Jesus saw in them and brought out latent and valuable talents that enabled them to create the Christian church, which would change the course of history in a decisive manner.

Throughout his history man has always been prone to fall into one fatal delusion, and that is to mistakenly perceive his own understanding of his real situation in history as being the correct one. The long span of history proves that God's teaching in the Bible is the reality-oriented outline of history, however much man's scholarship will tend to set it aside. Modern archeology has tended to confirm biblical details and substance which critics in a former day have discounted as being valid.

One of the apostles who can help us to orient ourselves properly in this scientific age—and his testimony is worthy of attention—is the Apostle Thomas. He demands our inspection; he initially had more courage (John 11:16) than Peter (John 18:15-27).

It is in the experience of Thomas that the reader can avoid one of the pitfalls of the modern era with its overwhelming intellectual

---

[4] *Ibid.*

pride and dazzlement with man's scientific progress. Historical tradition places Thomas as working to establish the church to the east of Palestine and into northern and western India. The question is, What convinced him of the risen Christ? From an analysis of his personality description, it could only have been the resurrected Christ. Jesus, while possessing some superhuman powers, yet had limited Himself to human form for all time, thus becoming our "elder brother." If there was no actual, real resurrection, then the whole Christian message might as well be dropped in the waste basket of history. The experience of Thomas the Apostle validates the reality of the Resurrection. Jesus made a point of having His apostles handle Him (John 20:27-28; Luke 24:39). The "doubting" of Matt. 28:17 sounds curiously genuine!

Since Jesus had bound Himself into humanity and was both an air breather and a being who needed to eat (Luke 22:18; 24:42-43; John 21:12-13), he left this planet in a different manner than He had arrived (Acts 1:9).

Jesus formulated certain principles by which one might enter His kingdom. He demands firstly a definite point of decision: man must turn wholly to God and enter into full fellowship with Him. "Jesus said to him. 'No one who puts his hand to the plow and looks back is fit for the kingdom of God'" (Luke 9:62). The number of people of the earth's populace past and present who will actually repent and obey is a minority.

Man's intrinsic arrogance and pride must be replaced by the relationship of child to father, for such we are before the grandeur of the Universal Intelligence, with all our 13 billion brain cells.

Jesus reduced all laws and stipulations to one—the law of love to God and love to one's neighbor (Mark 12:28). This totals man's behavioral guide. His kingdom is not of this world (John 18:36), and the Christian thus finds himself a citizen of an orderly, constructive, stable, interstellar, transgalactic civilization who happens to find himself on a planet in rebellion against the sovereign ruler of the universe—God.

Citizenship in this ideal and creative community is achieved by the unmerited mercy of God—grace—and by subsequent obedient discipleship made possible by the grace. Man must repent in true sorrow for sin and renounce it. He must believe in Christ and commit himself to Him as Saviour and Lord. This committed obedience must continue in faith unto death (Luke 14:26-27).

The Christian must act with love in social relations to do what can be done to alleviate suffering and distress in the world. The Christian's existential experience should be characterized by vitality, curiosity, and diligence, with a considerable dash of common sense thrown in.

Through nearly two thousand years the church has marched through history, advancing, retreating, with both success and failure at times having its share of heroes and traitors to the cause. During this time Israel was put on the shelf, so to speak, until 1948. Apparently the "full number of the Gentiles" is being approached in the latter half of the 20th century (Rom. 11:25).

The Second Coming of Christ has been predicted in many Scriptures in which He promises to come again (John 14:3; Rev. 22:20). With the fixation point of the end-time in 1948 and the subsequent development of certain prophecies that are shaping up in world history, we can see that there is no credibility gap with God. He is moving the schedule of historical events on time as promised. The doctrine of the Second Coming of Jesus Christ is today not only credible but extremely relevant to the development of any sane philosophy of history to understand the global mess mankind is creating. To find peace of mind in the latter part of the 20th century, man must take a "leap of faith," although the evidences available in our day and age surpass those our ancestors had access to as to the validity of the Bible and its prophetic message acting through time. Faith seen as unverified probability based on substantial evidence is an intellectually acceptable article. A century ago the idea that Israel would again be established as a nation seemed to most people preposterous, yet so has it happened. God has gathered His Chosen People in preparation for some final cosmic events in the history of the planet Earth.

In the long history of mankind only one Person emerges with the moral authority to bring peace out of disorder, sanity out of madness, and meaning out of folly. He was a man who was a worker, as a carpenter, in the true Marxian sense, fully Jewish as

COURTESY BRAUN ET CIE, DORNACH (HAUT-RHIN), FRANCE

A picture of the Apostles of Christ on Saturday after the Crucifixion and before the Resurrection. The only reality that could have changed this depressed, disheartened band of men into the activists that created the Christian church was the actual, physical, resurrected Christ. Nothing else can explain adequately the origin of Christianity. ("Holy Saturday"—Burnand.)

the "root of Jesse," yet bound to all humanity as a being like ourselves. He exercised authority and leadership as no other person ever has. He felt grief as we do (Matt. 7:34; Luke 6:41) and possibly got sawdust in His eyes on occasion. He had a sense of humor that is generally not appreciated and is unique in its handling of irony. When the priests and scribes sought to put Him on the spot in asking about John the Baptist (Luke 20:1-8), they found that they had been placed there instead. The crowd must have chuckled about that exchange. Irony characterized Christ's wit without the desire to wound which epitomizes sarcasm. Jesus could and did rebuke with firmness and authority when needed (Luke 16:23). The humorous point of the parable of the crooked servant in Luke 16:1-15 is a joking harpooning of the greedy idea that one can steal big and go to heaven too. Some interpreters have worked hard to extract a moralistic teaching from this story without seeing it for what it is—a bit of humor.

How is the "new birth" of which Jesus spoke to Nicodemus effected? This is the process that reconciles man to God through Christ (Rom. 5:11). Here we deal with matters of faith, yet one can visualize that on a biophysical level the Holy Spirit, an extra-anthropomorphic form of God that is present on Earth, can somehow both perceive our thinking and impress thoughts upon us. In some subtle manner our nature is changed to enable us to function as better moral beings, a process that seems to consist in something more than an intellectual assent to belief. Since the brain is constantly emitting electromagnetic waves, this can be seen as quite a reasonable idea. Somehow the defective nature of mankind is changed or regenerated by God's grace to enable man to live again the kind of orderly, loving, creative existence originally intended by God. A new soul is processed through the personality expression; a complete understanding of this event may never be reached by man, but the effects are observable. Men's lives are changed by accepting Christ. These changes nullify the attempts of behavioral scientists to explain "conversions" as simply the result of psychological factors.

In the new life style of the redeemed person certain patterns have been ordained as proper and moral, basic integrity being foremost. Sexuality is to be confined within the married state, in which unashamed passionate desire should be expressed (S. of S. 7:1-9). Aggression is to be modulated with ethical concern for one's fellow man, and acquisitiveness is to be kept within the bounds of common sense (I Tim. 6:10, 17-19). The mode of living, then, for the follower of Christ is as expressed by a Quaker some centuries ago:

> *. . . having God's fear in our hearts that we may keepe our consciences clear before him from whom we receive strength to uphould us in tryalls . . . that we live a peaceable, holy and godlike life.*

The Christian can face the troubles and turmoils of the modern era with considerable equanimity. Even death does not hold the anxiety for him that it holds for the person who knows not God. In that ultimate day at the end of the church era, God will correct the whole situation in accordance with the purposes of the moral universe He has created and sustains.

The increasing lawlessness breaking out in the world in the 1960-70 decades is social anarchy that does not basically derive from faulty social structure, but derives rather from the results of individual life styles. The cumulative effect of the alienation from God's will by many individuals results in a nonviable global social order. In view of the increasing instability of the duration of individual life on this world, it behooves each person to remember that death is the ultimate reality he may face any day and therefore for him, "Behold, *now* is the *day* of salvation," (II Cor. 6:2) and not to delay a decision to choose to serve God. Scripture symbolically portrays those who refuse the generous unmerited grace of God paid for by the atoning death of Jesus:

> *"For if we sin deliberately after receiving the knowledge of the truth, there no longer remains a sacrifice for sins, but a fearful prospect of judgment, and a fury of fire which will consume the adversaries" (Heb. 10:26-27).*

Before those who fail to accept Christ lies also a future whose eventual exact biophysical state of existence is not easy to define except to say that it will be one of separation from God, a lonely divisiveness, anguish, guilt, and punishment by a just God for evil done in this life. In the end the "second death" will occur, and the effect of evil will be eradicated from the universe.

It is my conclusion based on many years of study that Jesus of Nazareth was exactly who He said He was—the Son of God, the Christ, and the Redeemer of mankind. For those who will accept Him, He is the only hope in this world for identity preservation in the salvation and eternal life He has promised.

10 A PROBABLE SCENARIO

With the reestablishment of Israel in 1948 and the ingathering of the Chosen People a "second time" (Isa. 11:10-12), the marking point of the end-time was fixed. Therefore it becomes appropriate to pull from the dusty shelves of theological seminaries the expositions of ancient eschatological prophecies, because they now become of practical importance for the Christian to understand.

It is of value to review a chart prepared by Rev. Clarence Larkin in 1918 and published in an excellent book delineating biblical teaching in useful and graphic illustrations. Larkin was both a minister of the gospel and a trained mechanical engineer who had a special genius for translating biblical prophecies and their concepts into chart form. His Chart No. 3 is reproduced here as being worthy of study, since it is a clear exposition of most of the biblical teaching concerning certain end-time events.

Larkin's chart is deserving of careful perusal. Looking at it from left to right, the reader will note the First Coming of Christ and the dispersal of Israel, which happened in A.D. 70, when the Roman legions took Jerusalem. Following this, the Church Age is depicted in a large oval. One notes at the bottom of the chart Israel being regathered (1948) before the end-time events. After Israel is reborn, the Rapture events, including the First Resurrection, are depicted. Then, within the half-circle dome, is the Tribulation period. Larkin's placement of some of the prophetic symbols may not be in agreement with that of all interpreters; however, it is in general. The seven Trumpets of Revelation 8, consisting of various signs in the natural world, will begin to herald the Second Coming of Christ, the rightful Sovereign of this planet. As the evil world empire is consolidated and seeks to finally destroy all

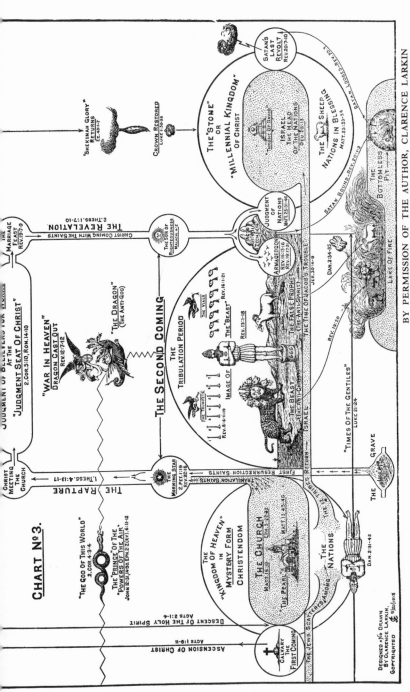

BY PERMISSION OF THE AUTHOR, CLARENCE LARKIN

A graphic portrayal of the history of God's purpose for His people both Jew and Gentile. This chart made over 50 years ago shows a striking parallel with events shaping up in the latter part of the 20th century.

who call upon the name of Christ for salvation and to destroy Israel, God will pour out upon the earth the seven last plagues, as shown in the chart. This manifestation of God's wrath upon a sinful world that has rejected His mercies will solve the population problem of Earth in short order as millions are swept away. Then will come pestilence, water pollution, drought, hail, and other calamities outlined in Rev. 16:1-21:

> *"Go and pour out on the earth the seven bowls of the wrath of God. . . . and foul and evil sores came upon the men who bore the mark of the beast and worshiped its image . . . to prepare the way for the kings from the east [China]. . . . And they assembled them at the place which is called in Hebrew Armageddon . . . and a great earthquake such as had never been since men were on the earth . . . and the cities of the nations fell. . . ."*

Larkin then shows the Battle of Armageddon with the Second Coming, followed by the establishment of the Millennial Kingdom. Concerning this end-time period of Tribulation upon the earth the prophet Daniel wrote to his people of Israel as follows:

> *"At that time shall Michael stand up, the great Prince who standeth for the children of thy people; and there shall be a time of trouble such as never was since there was a nation . . . and at that time thy people shall be delivered, every one that shall be found written in the book. And many of them that sleep in the dust of the earth shall awake, some to everlasting life. . . ." (Dan. 12:1-2)*

At this period of time, when Israel faces the massed armies of the earth, she will not stand alone, for God has the whole power of the universe to succor her. And so He shall do. The reader is encouraged to check the biblical references in Larkin's chart and note also its date of origin, 1918.

The one question that Winston Churchill asked Rev. Billy Graham when they met was, "Do you see any hope for the world?" That hope, the Second Coming of Jesus Christ, is the only reality that can offer men any solid footing to erect a sane society on this planet. During the 1970s lawlessness will increase to the extent that democratic governments everywhere will gradually be changed to fascist structures. Although this will be a later development in America, it will eventually come. Dr. Bruno Bettleheim of the University of Chicago, a man who spent a year in one of Hitler's concentration camps, has correctly pointed out that there is a striking resemblance between the violence breaking out in America today and the violence that he witnessed in Germany just prior to the rise to power of Hitler. Fascism, when it comes in the United States, will be wrapped in the American flag but will still be a dictatorship. It may arrive in the late 1970s or early 1980s, but arrive it will. The decade of the 1970s will probably be evidenced by a continual degradation in national dignity in America which will prepare the way for a change from democracy to an authoritarian regime. The social conditions in America in the 1960s and those preceding the fall of the Roman Republic are strikingly similar. Many persons cannot or do not wish to accept the idea that the shining "patriot's dream" of America with its wonderful freedoms unequaled in human history will pass away. I must regretfully point out that human governments are only as good as the men who make them up and that both are subject to moral decay. A certain political candidate for President in 1968 may have been a frightening straw in the wind. Should increasing urban decay, environmental pollution, lawlessness, crime, and inflation culminate in a crisis after World War III, then fascism can come to America.

A recent study by the Research Survey Center of the University of California regarding anti-Semitism and released in 1969 shows that more than one-third of the American population are passively anti-Semitic and another one-half are apathetic toward discrimination against Jews. Scarcely one-sixth of the population are consistent opponents of anti-Semitism on the basis of principle. The social situation therefore exists, as Dore Schary has pointed out, for the rise to political power in America of an anti-Semitic candidate with a promised economic solution during a crisis period.

This is what may happen in America in the 1980s, and it would fit in with God's overall plan to regather His Chosen People by moving the large segment in America out of "Babylon" back to Israel.

Increasing lawlessness in the entire world will make the rise of a powerful world leader inevitable in order to bring the social chaos to an end by utilizing the one method that can unify unregenerate persons—force and terror!

When one plots the "time span" of the period 1962-1999, the period of life and activity of the world leader seen by Mrs. Dixon on a chart of probable events in the second half of the 20th century, several interesting phenomena become apparent.

In the spring of 1969 a most surprising speech was made by Lin Piao, Defense Minister of China. He stated that China must make preparations against the possibility of the United States and the Soviet Union launching a nuclear war directed against China. This statement indicates a remarkable shift in attitude in the international community between two Communist nations who once exchanged expressions of "eternal friendship."

The Committee on Atomic Energy of the U.S. Congress estimated in a 1967 report that China would have an operational intercontinental ballistic missile capability by 1972.

During the 1970s the ICBM strike force of the Chinese will continue to grow and create ever-mounting concern in both Russia and the West. Other weaponry previously discussed is being developed, so that mass death can be produced by means other than atomic weapons.

One can expect that UFO activity will continue during the 1970s, with more Christians becoming aware of its true significance. A New Zealand National Airlines pilot, Captain Bruce Cathie, has shown by careful analysis that the UFOs seem to be establishing and using a navigational "grid" which is the same in New Zealand as in other parts of the world. This may constitute preparation for the work described in Mark 13:26-27. With the dawn of man's own Space Age, a more accurate clarification of just what kind of "cloud" Jesus will return to this earth in becomes available.

China and African nations will draw closer together as China assists revolutionary regimes in Africa with an increasing supply of weapons. China will probably gain more influence with the Arab nations as Russia turns to the West for security. At such times those evangelists who have been astute enough to refrain from useless anti-Russian polemics may be able to do some evangelistic work in the USSR. David Ben-Gurion has advanced the thesis, which is probably valid, that when Russia turns to the West, she will allow her Jewish citizens to leave for Israel. This, of course, would fit in with God's sovereign plan of ingathering His Chosen People in preparation for the climactic events of world history. Some persons who view the present pro-Arab, anti-Israeli stance of the Soviet government as a fixed position are forgetting that national attitudes may change and indeed that the USSR actually aided in the initial recognition of Israel by the UN.

During the 1970-80s churches will move more and more into merger-type arrangements which will eventuate in the 1990s in the world apostate church, a church in which a kind of bland, nondemanding humanism will replace the "new birth" spoken of by the Lord Jesus as necessary for entrance into His kingdom. Signs of this adulteration of the true gospel are already appearing in the Christian church in the 1960s. As a trained behavioral scientist I have viewed with some astonishment the naiveté of certain clergymen and churchmen in their attempts to utilize sociological schemes to change human behavior. These attempts are in contradiction to the specific program of the Lord Jesus, who pointed out that the way for entrance into fellowship with God was by a "new" interpersonal relationship given to man as a gift and maintained by God's grace. Force is the only cement that can create a unified society out of unregenerate persons. To admit that one needs to cast oneself on God's mercy as a child of His rubs against the primary narcissism of mankind, hence the search for other "gospels" in our modern day and age. For social acts to be meaningful in the Christian sense, they must be derived from a primary personal relationship with Jesus Christ.

During the 1970s the world population will continue to rise essentially unchecked by the ineffectual schemes of democratic governments to control it. The crisis point will be reached about 1980, more or less. At this point the food resources of the world will have reached a point where famines begin to break out in some nations and regions. The pressure of hunger will cause World War III to break out, with China and parts of Africa attacking the West and its ally Russia. Toynbee's concept that

An intercontinental ballistic missile base. One such nuclear-bomb missile can reduce a large modern city to a smoking ruin in minutes. The US and the USSR have hundreds of these missiles, ready for firing at a moment's notice. China will have its first ICBM about 1973.

And Jesus said, ". . . you will hear of wars and rumors of wars; see that you are not alarmed; for this must take place, but the end is not yet" (Matt. 24:6).

COURTESY MARTIN MARIETTA CORP.

the Russian empire will shelter itself with the West against the onslaught of the Chinese civilization would seem to be valid, and indeed in 1969 bloody border clashes broke out between Russian and Chinese troops, an omen of things to come.

World War III will be horrendous. A significant portion of the world's population will be killed. Probably either Vietnam or Korea will be the flash point from which the war will start. The initial phase of the war will probably be one of great cunning, with the use of new bacteriological weapons in an attempt to seize land and resources by population destruction alone. It probably will quickly escalate into a nuclear-missile contest, and the loss of life will be fearful. Many modern cities will cease to exist, as did Hiroshima.

Amidst the wreckage of their various civilizations after World War III the earthpeople will become desperate for some kind of security in their lives, and the stage will be set for two major developments of world history in the 1980s. It is in 1983 that the world leader seen by Mrs. Dixon as having been born in the 1960s will reach maturity. The time of his maturation when coupled with the global geopolitical conditions in the 1980s mark him as the long-anticipated Antichrist.

When Hitler rose to power, a noted German Christian leader, Pastor Martin Niemöller, perceptively commented, "Verily a time of sifting has come upon us. God is giving Satan a free hand, so that he may shake us up and so that it may be seen what manner of men we are." Other churchmen were not so perceptive, and one made the statement, "Christ has come to us through Adolf Hitler." The total record of the Christian church in Germany is a spotty one and nothing to brag about. It was another example of some Christians' mistakenly committing the sin of idolatry by rendering unto Caesar what belonged to God. Christians of a later generation had better ponder the example of the German church well.

During the 1980s as the Antichrist world dictator comes onto the stage of history, statements of equal idiocy will be made by some churchmen.

Those churchmen in America who are unwisely attempting to

PHOTOWORLD—FPG

The same idolatrous adulation that was accorded Hitler in this monster rally in Nazi Germany will be accorded the world dictator in the 1990-2000 period. Those inhabitants of earth who worship the Antichrist and receive his mark ultimately find that they have bought a one-way ticket to Hell. The new "swastika" (mark) might conceivably be something like this:

A modern-day "peace" symbol, this was cited by the well-known Protestant theologian John Knox as the "mark of the beast" after its use in the Middle Ages by anti-Christian groups. Its form dates back to the Roman Empire, when Nero crucified the Apostle Peter on an upside-down cross with broken arms.

destroy the wall of separation of church and state so that they can "improve society" will ultimately find that if they are successful, they will have created a monster that will devour them. As Santayana has remarked, "Those who will not learn the lessons of history are condemned to repeat them." Any attempt to fuse church and state in America allegedly "under God" will simply erect another idolatrous nationalistic image for man to worship.

The nominal religious person believes that everybody in the world will be converted, and he works in various ways to effect this. The biblical view is, as previously stated, that God has effected a rescue operation on this planet and will "take out . . . a people for his name" (Acts 15:14; Rom. 11:25). Therefore in the next two decades the percentage of true followers of Jesus in relation to the world population may actually decline slightly.

With his symbolic origin in Egypt the Antichrist may well be the leader of a pan-Arabic federation whose relative power position on the international scene will have been enhanced by the decline in power of the West, Russia, and China by the damaging effects of World III. He will advance brilliant solutions to desperate international problems, and a desperate world will surrender its individual freedoms in return for security, a trade not without precedent in history. During the 1980s there will emerge a gradual consolidation of global political organizations. Slowly but surely power will be centralized under the rulership of this one man, who will initially appear as a benevolent despot. The United Nations may become his base of operations. Christians who know their biblical prophecy thoroughly will not be fooled by this man; others will. The same adulation accorded Hitler in Nazi Germany will be accorded this man. He will resolve the pressing food-shortage problem in time of global famine; hence the symbolic reference to "Joseph," who did the same for seven years in the land of Egypt so long ago. A worldwide system of computerized identification with food rationing will probably be instituted.

As a result of the suffering of World War III mankind will in anguish of heart turn from its various idols, such as technology, progress, money, education, and power, and many will seek the one true God. The 1980 decade will be one of unparalleled

END TIME FLOW CHART

Copyright Charles D. Willis, 1972

CHRIST

The reader can see at a glance that the convergence of various historical processes, as has never occurred before in the history of the world, is setting the stage for the Second Coming of Christ. The probable events in the last third of the 20th century are a fulfillment of Jesus' words in Luke 21:24-28. God is not only alive and well but is developing exactly on schedule the historical events so long prophesied. If the Antichrist assumes full world power at the age of 30 years in imitation of Jesus (Luke 3:23), he will do so about 1992, an approximate point in time that may mark the Rapture event. The Second Coming should happen some time before or during Israel's Year of Jubilee, 1998.

ANTICHRIST

evangelistic opportunity as the message of Christ is given forth to reap a harvest before the Rapture event.

With global telecommunications systems available in the 1980s, the gospel of Christ will be presented on a worldwide basis as never before in the history of mankind. Many will be converted and enter into His kingdom and life eternal (Matt. 24:14).

Because of the pressing food/population crisis, governments in the 1980s will become increasingly authoritarian. The world dictator will succeed in unifying them into one, possibly through the United Nations. Some church leaders will mistakenly cooperate with this world leader, since he will seem to be benevolent in attitude initially, until he obtains supreme power over the world. Other church leaders will astutely recognize him for who he really is.

An End Time Flow Chart, when constructed, shows a striking similarity to Rev. Mr. Larkin's prophetic interpretation done over fifty years ago. The end-time prophecy calls for the reestablishment of Israel, to be followed by world conditions which will "cause men fainting with fear and with foreboding of what is coming on the world" (Luke 21:26). The prospects of global atomic war, famine, and social deterioration are fast fulfilling Jesus' words as the decade of the 1970s opens. Dealing with the historical phenomena in sequence it can be seen that the evil government of Hitler was a warning to the world of what will occur during the reign of the Antichrist. Christian people tend to forget that Hitler's regime was anti-Christian as well as anti-Jewish and that he killed over seven million Christians as well as five million Jews. In an excellent chapter "The Brown Shirted Christ Killers," Max Dimont has graphically sketched in his *Jews, God and History* the evil mechanism that propelled Hitler to power. He correctly identifies the fact that the basic anti-Christianity of German Nazism has been almost totally overlooked by journalists and historians. It is to this example that Christians must look if they wish to understand the conditions of the Tribulation period. Nazism was not just anti-Semitic; it was anti-human.

If one conceptualizes the idea that the Antichrist will counterfeit and imitate Jesus, who began His ministry when He was thirty years of age (Luke 3:23), then a most interesting correlation develops when one deducts thirty years from the period 1962-1999, because seven years are left. Seven years have long been predicted as the period of time when the Antichrist will rule the world with total power, and the time period delineated by Mrs. Dixon fits into the global historical scheme.

If the Rapture event is to be just before the seven-year reign, it should happen about 1992. The reason for the UFO activity starting in the late 1940s may become apparent if the "clouds" which will remove the followers of Christ from this world materialize as a vast fleet of spaceships to take those who are saved to other worlds throughout the universe (John 14:2-3). Probably at this very moment crews of "angels" on other worlds are carefully studying reconnaisance data of this planet preparatory to the events connected with the Second Coming. The Rapture is generally predicted as a supernatural event, since the resurrection of the righteous will occur, to be followed quickly by the changing of the defective bodies of those still alive who are Christ's true disciples into perfect bodies. An electromagnetic event of considerable scope and finesse on the part of God! There may be a natural aspect to it also in terms of the extraterrestrial transportation system, hence the preliminary appearance of UFO activity over the earth. Some interpreters have thought that the Rapture event will be "secret" and simultaneous over the entire earth (Luke 17:34-35). Those who are left behind will only perceive that a certain portion of the population has vanished, having been snapped into some different time-space continuum. This may not be entirely true, but whatever the exact details of this event it will be a time of great joy for the redeemed as they meet Christ personally and are reunited with loved ones. In any event the Lord Jesus will approach the earth with His space force (I Thess. 4:16-17; John 5:28-29), and perhaps at His shout of command, "My people, come forth!" the redeemed dead "in Christ" will rise to eternal life as He promised. The translation of the living redeemed will also occur, and His people will be removed from this planet.

During the seven years, if the pre-tribulational concept of the

Rapture is correct, the redeemed will be in "heavenly places" (Eph. 3:10) receiving a judgment for works done as a fruit of salvation obtained through the grace of God. One might speculate, for instance, that Dr. David Livingstone might be rewarded for his part in the work of the gospel by being named viceroy of Scotland in the Millennial Kingdom; Father Damien might become governor of Hawaii. These "heavenly places" will probably include thousands of planets (John 14:2-3) which are even now being prepared for the arrival of the earthpeople. Since America's astronauts landed on the moon in 1969 it becomes very easy to visualize such a situation. In some manner the Antichrist world dictator will in the late 1980s or early 1990s deal with the question of Israel in the Mideast and offer to conclude a covenant, or treaty, with her allegedly ensuring her safety.

The Israelis will get what they most want now, a high-sounding international treaty which will seemingly guarantee the security of the land of Israel and its people. During this time a further ingathering of Jews of the world may proceed. The leaders of Israel will, with some exceptions, mistakenly perceive the world dictator as a friend and perhaps as a Messiah. Hopefully all the leaders of Israel will be fully alert to the evil and seductive character of this person and make an alternate decision. Between now and then all Christians should make it their duty to inform their Jewish friends in a friendly and factual manner that the Second Coming is approaching and of the true character of the Antichrist. If the leaders of Israel will rely not upon the arm of flesh, the reed of Egypt, and the strength of men and their treaties, then the time of Jacob's trouble predicted for Israel may be averted, in accordance with the promise of Jer. 18:5-12 and Ex. 19:5.

The correct decision for the nation of Israel to make at that time would be to have its leaders call for a period of national fasting, repentance, and consecration to the God of their fathers. If this is done and Israel calls upon God to deliver them, then the arrival of their Messiah and the establishment of the kingdom will be speeded up.

The Bible also indicates that a false prophet will help the

Antichrist to assume power over the world. No doubt he will be on international television promising to all everything that they want in life, and then some. Anyone who believes him will make a serious error in historical judgment. As the power of the world dictator grows to its ultimate height, about 1992, the Rapture event will probably take place if it is to precede the absolutist rule of the Antichrist during the seven-year period predicted in many places.

When the Rapture occurs, about 1992, and many Christians disappear, Jewish people, their curiosity intensely aroused, will search the New Testament anew for an explanation. There are biblical indications that many will realize that Jesus of Nazareth was truly their Messiah and bear witness to God and His Christ (Rev. 7:1-8; 11:3-13). As the Rapture is concluding they also may see Christ's space fleet orbiting earth before it departs from our solar system.

The Rapture will leave on earth those who are unconverted in heart and mind, those in essential rebellion against God. As evil assumes complete control over the world the immoral climate that exists will create again the days of Sodom and Gomorrah. Drugs, greed, brutality, and so-called sexual freedom on a scale never before seen will characterize the social structure of the world state. There will be no love and no trust between persons. Those activities which are beginning to destroy the social fabric of America in the 1960s will be indulged in with increasing frequency and excess. In the end people will reap as they sow. From the period 1992-1995 a pseudo peace will exist in the world at the cost of individual freedom. Man will become, as in the novel *1984*, the slave of the state. The price of existence in such a world state will be complete obedience to the will of the world dictator. No economic activity will be carried on by anyone not having an ID card, available for checking by a computer the mark signifying their allegiance to and worship of the world leader. As a consequence of their act of belief in Jesus Christ as Lord and Saviour, Christians will now suffer death when they refuse to worship the Antichrist. They will join some of their brothers in the days of the Caesars of ancient Rome who died before they would worship

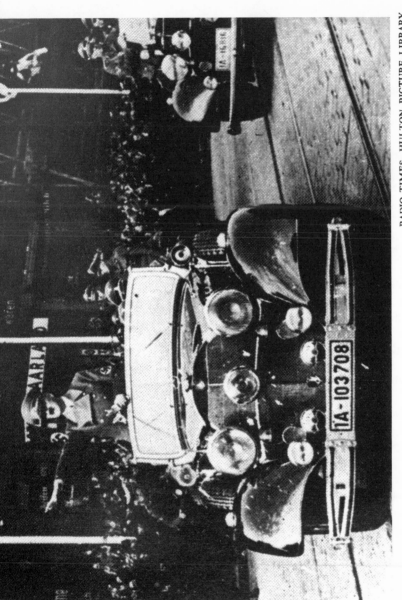

Adolf Hitler in his early days of triumph and power. When he took over the German government in 1933, General Ludendorff accurately wrote to President Hindenburg: "I predict most solemnly that this man will die in incredible misery. Coming generations will curse you for naming him Chancellor." The Antichrist world dictator will meet a similar fa·

the emperor. Some biblical interpreters have thought that the first half of the seven-year reign of the Antichrist will be a peaceful one and that the persecutory extermination of Christians will not start until the middle of that period. Time will tell. During this period of time the great "whore" who sits upon the "beast" will be constituted. An apostate church lacking true piety will support the Antichrist. This situation is pictured in Revelation 17 and 18. Amalgamation of church and state will, as has happened in the past, lead to a corruption of religious belief and practice. During the 1970-80s a continual erosion of papal authority will take place. This development will open the way for a further consolidation of the apostate world church, which will have the form of Christianity without the substance. Some church leaders will mistakenly co-operate with the Antichrist, and God will call the honest in heart "out of" this false ecclesiastical structure. The Antichrist may show great signs and wonders with unusual cunning and intelligence, perhaps even claim to be the returned Christ. However, the Lord Jesus was very specific in stating how He would return to this planet:

> *"For false Christs and false prophets will arise and show great signs and wonders, so as to lead astray, if possible, even the elect. Lo, I have told you beforehand. . . . For as the lightning comes from the east and shines as far as the west, so will be the coming of the Son of man." (Matt. 24:24-27.)*

Finally the Antichrist will demand that the populace of earth worship him as a god, an action for which there exist numerous precedents in human history, the adoration formerly accorded the emperor of Japan within this century being the most recent example. He will demand that Israel worship his "image" in Jerusalem, where the Third Temple may have been erected by that time. The "image" to the beast (Rev. 13) which "lived" can also be understood symbolically as the social system which the Antichrist will structure in his world empire and which will be a reflection of his own evil philosophy. This system, like Nazism, will seem viable to the deluded world populace and will appeal to mankind's pride and arrogance to deceive men into accepting the idea that they can be

A UFO seen by Brazilian naval and air force officers on the ship *Almirante Saldanha* and photographed by A. Barauna, who happened to be on the deck. The UFO came in over Trinidade Island in early 1958. Photograph released by President Kubitschek of Brazil. A primitive people might have misinterpreted this vehicle, which is obviously of artificial design and construction, as a "cloud."

their own saviour. The subtle allusion to the smashing of this false world empire via Christ's return in Dan. 2:35 should not be lost on the reader. There are precedents in Jewish history for such a situation if one remembers Antiochus and Caligula. The Jews will refuse the idolatrous demand for worship, and prophecy indicates that they will endure the "time of Jacob's trouble" (Mark 13:14; Jer. 30:3; Matt. 24:21) as the Antichrist invades Israel to seek to destroy her. By this time, the midpoint of the seven-year reign of the world dictator, about 1995, true Christians, with some exceptions, will have been the victims of the "final solution," namely, extermination. Rev. 20:4 "Also I saw the souls of those who had been beheaded . . . and who had not worshiped the beast or its image and had not received its mark on their foreheads or their hands. They came to life, and reigned with Christ a thousand years." The period of time during which the Antichrist is allowed to act is limited. To bring trial upon Israel and the rest of the world he has no more than three and one-half years, biblically mentioned in several places ("the middle of the week"—Dan. 9:27; "forty-two months"—Rev. 11:2; 13:5; and 1260 days"— Rev. 11:3; 12:6). These prophetic indicators that show God's limiting sovereignty over the beast are a hopeful point for the people of Israel and the Tribulation saints to remember. If it were not for the prophetic light of the Bible, earthpeople might think that the power of evil might continue indefinitely in a triumphant posture over our world. Such is not to be the case.

The people of Israel will experience at this time the refining test of loyalty to God as described in Zech. 13:9: " 'And I will put this third into the fire, and refine them as one refines silver, and test them as gold is tested. They will call on my name, and I will answer them. I will say, 'They are my people'; and they will say, 'The Lord is my God.' " Some Israeli citizens have mistakenly thought that they can be Jews while being atheists. This is a delusion, as history will show. *God cannot be left out of the equation of world history!*

Many Gentiles will call upon the name of the Lord during this trying period. They are described in Rev. 7:9-14: ". . . behold, a great multitude which no man could number, from every nation,

The great Andromeda Galaxy with its millions of solar systems and innumerable worlds. Traveling faster than the speed of light will come Christ's space force from far-distant "heavenly places" to effect the events of the Second Coming.

from all tribes and peoples . . . 'These are they who have come out of the great tribulation; they have washed their robes and made them white in the blood of the Lamb.' " Human political leaders of the earth commonly seek to dampen or attenuate polarization within their national societies. However, the intention of God working in the last days of earth's history is to foster and produce a sharp point of polarization for mankind to use its power of authentic choice to decide between good and evil, for God or against Him. As the Antichrist invades the Middle East and the Holy Land, Israel will resist his armies with partial success, but Jerusalem will suffer damage. Now will come upon the earth the period of the Great Tribulation. Upon an unrepentant, unregenerate world God will now deliver some overdue punishments, and the seven last plagues will strike the earth. The ecological balance of food resources and population hunger will be so delicately controlled in the 1990s that any interference with social organization by any event will create worldwide chaos. Various troubles will strike the earth, such as pestilence, famine, thirst, and drought. The Gonyloux organism will probably proliferate in the oceans, destroying a large share of one of mankind's major sources of food. A great global earthquake will wreak havoc over the entire world, changing the shape of continents. The resultant global catastrophes will terrify mankind. Some people even in this day of judgments will repent and accept Christ as Saviour and Lord, although to do so will be very difficult.

The leaders of the world empire will sense the impending return of Christ to claim His rightful kingdom, and the Antichrist will marshal his terrestrial armed forces to complete the destruction of Israel. The anti-Christian world state may control all the armies converging upon Israel, or the empire may break up and the various world civilizations fight each other, due to the events of the Tribulation period, with the Middle East as the final battleground. The vast armies of the Sinic civilization will be there (Rev. 16:12), as will others. The Antichrist will want not only to destroy the Chosen People but also to contest Christ's sovereign right to rule over the earth. A delusion will possess mankind to the effect that they will actually think that they can resist the power of God and

A view of the earth that some of the pilots of Christ's space force (Rev. 1:7) will have as they make their final approach to rendezvous in the skies over our planet to effect both the Rapture event and the Second Coming. Then the redeemed of earth will come to know the reality of the promise of Jesus: "In my Father's house are many rooms; if it were not so, would I have told you that I go to prepare a place for you? And when I go and prepare a place for you, I will come again and will take you to myself, that where I am you may be also." (John 14:2-3.)

His Christ when He returns to claim and exercise His authority over the earth. Mankind will be unified at this time by hate, an unstable cement, rather than love, which endures for all time. (II Thess. 2:9-12).

In ancient Israel a custom of designating every fiftieth year as a year in which those in bondage were freed was established by Moses. It was formulated (Lev. 25:28) as a means of helping the covenant people find their redeemer during a year of freedom and grace, and was called the Year of Liberty (Ezek. 46:17). According to the words of Christ himself, the Antichrist will not be permitted to reign for the full seven years, 1992-1999, since the Tribulation will be "shortened" (Matt. 24:21-22). It is interesting to note that if the Second Coming occurs in 1997 or 1998, it will coincide with the fiftieth anniversary year of Israel—the Year of Jubilee—and therefore correlates typologically.

As the military forces of the Antichrist seek to destroy Israel completely a great army will converge toward the Middle East. When all hope seems gone, Christ will appear with His space force (Rev. 1:7) and engage the terrestrial armed forces of the world in the Battle of Armageddon, thus rescuing Israel (Matt. 23:39; 24:15-31). Christ's forces, backed by all the power of the universe, will seize control of the whole planet in one simultaneous act known in military parlance as a total on-time-attack operation. The war of the Sons of Light with the Sons of Darkness will at this point in time bring to a final end the "times of the Gentiles."

A total immobilization of every military structure on the planet Earth will occur so that no one will contest the will of the Lord Jesus. A destruction of the evil armies of earth will ensue and of wicked men everywhere (Luke 19:27). In accordance with II Thess. 1:5-10, a sociological cleansing of the earth will be accomplished as warlords, criminals, members of the Mafia, and other evildoers are therapeutically exterminated in justice. They may attempt to hide and call upon "the mountains and the rocks" (Rev. 6:16-17) to enable them to elude Christ's forces, but this will be a vain hope and delusion. Now some men will feel the anguish of "what might have been" as they realize they are not included in Christ's kingdom and will never enjoy the wonders of

A view of the planet Earth that the pilots of Christ's powerful space fleet will have as they plunge toward our world to rendezvous in the skies over the Holy Land to engage the armed forces of the Antichrist in combat in the Battle of Armageddon, thus rescuing Israel. "O Jerusalem, Jerusalem . . . you will not see me again until you say, 'Blessed be he who comes in the name of the Lord!'" Thus spoke Jesus nearly 2,000 years ago (Matt. 23:37-39).

eternal life in loving fellowship with God. Some will be those of His Chosen People who were not loyal to the covenant of their fathers and they will with others "weep and gnash their teeth" (Matt. 8: 11-12) as they realize Whittier's truth, "Of all sad words of tongue or pen, the saddest are these: 'It might have been!' "

At this point the redeemed who have been martyred during the Tribulation period will be resurrected (Rev. 6:9-11; 7:13-14), and great will be their joy (Ps. 68:3) as they rejoin loved ones. Great also will be Jesus' own joy as He takes command of His kingdom, something for which He has waited a long time. Jude, the younger half-brother of Jesus, sensed and pointed out this human quality of our Lord that we tend to overlook (Jude 24). Now will dawn for the inhabitants of the world the long-awaited Millennial Kingdom of Christ. He will rule the earth in person and establish the government of the world upon principles of truth,

© 1966 UNITED FEATURES SYNDICATE, INC.
The terrestrial armed forces of the Antichrist world dictator in the 1990s will meet the same fate as the snowmen of Linus. The days of the Antichrist are numbered!

honor, dignity, and social justice, perhaps with the kibbutz as a partial model. The redeemed of all ages will rule with Him; and in the thousand years to follow, mankind will see God pour out blessings upon earth without measure. The joy and goodness of abundant creative living will be so great that former sorrows will be remembered without anguish. Israel will then be the leading nation of the earth, and the promise made to Abraham will be fulfilled (Gen. 22:17-18). During the millennium certain technological advances may be anticipated, such as transgalactic television and interplanetary travel, in a peaceful society based on justice and love. In addition "no eye has seen, nor ear heard, nor the heart of man conceived, what God has prepared for those who love him" (I Cor. 2:9; Rev. 7:17).

It is not my intention to move beyond this point in time, as has been done in other studies. The important point is, my reader, are you a follower of the Lord Jesus Christ? He died to effect for you the retrieval of the destiny of eternal life originally designed by God for you. If you will now seek Him, find Him, and accept Him in a personal relationship of salvation and acknowledge Him as Saviour and Lord, then we shall meet in the coming kingdom.

I do not propose, nor should the reader propose, to fix exactly in point of time the actual Rapture event or Second Coming, since this is known only to God the Father (Matt. 24:36). At the same time, the Lord Jesus specifically directed us in Luke 21:28 as follows:

> *"Now when these things begin to take place, look up and raise your heads, because your redemption is drawing near."*

This may be construed as a subtle allusion to the UFO phenomenon, but also as a clear direction to the effect that it is possible to have a clearer understanding of approximately when these events will happen if one takes care to note the events of history-fulfilling prophecy. The construction of the thesis outlined in this study is therefore done with these words of Christ in mind, and hopefully is illuminating for the reader. I have eliminated some details of the situation which may be found in other sources and have attempted to present the "big picture."

"For God so loved the world that he gave his only Son, that whoever believes in him should not perish but have eternal life. For God sent the Son into the world, not to condemn the world, but that the world might be saved through him." [John 3:16-17]

"He has showed you, O man, what is good; and what does the Lord require of you but to do justice, and to love kindness, and to walk humbly with your God?" [Mic. 6:8]

"And when he had said this, as they were looking on, He was lifted up, and a cloud took him out of their sight. . . . This Jesus, who was taken up from you into heaven, will come in the same way as you saw him go into heaven." [Acts 1:9-11]

Jesus said . . . "I am the resurrection and the life; he who believes in me, though he die, yet shall he live, and whoever lives and believes in me shall never die." [John 11:25-26]

"They shall be mine, says the Lord of hosts, my special possession on the day when I act, and I will spare them as a man spares his son who serves him. Then once more you shall distinguish between one who serves God and one who does not serve him." [Mal. 3:17-18]

"A new commandment I give to you, that you love one another; even as I have loved you, that you also love one another. By this all men will know that you are my disciples, if you have love for one another." [John 13:34-35]

BIBLIOGRAPHY

1. PREPARATION

The Holy Bible, R.S.V. New York, Nelson, 1952.
Toynbee, Arnold J., *A Study of History,* Abridged, Vols. I & II, London, Oxford Univ. Press, 1957.

2. ISRAEL: PAST, PRESENT AND FUTURE

Eban, Abba, *My People: The Story of the Jews,* New York, Behrman House, & Random House, 1968.
Dimont, Max, *Jews, God and History.* New York, Signet Books, 1962.
Michener, James, *The Source.* New York, Random House, 1965.
Orr, William W., *Can the Jew Survive?* Wheaton, Ill., Scripture Press, 1961.
Robinson, Donald, *Under Fire: Israel's 20 Year Struggle for Survival.* New York, W. W. Norton, 1968.
Stevenson, William, *Strike Zion.* New York, Bantam Books, 1967.
Walvoord, John F., *Israel in Prophecy.* Grand Rapids, Mich., Zondervan, 1962.
Wolff, Richard, *Israel, Act III.* Wheaton, Ill., Tyndale House, 1967.

3. UNIDENTIFIED FLYING OBJECTS

Committee of Science & Astronautics, *Symposium on U.F.O.s,* U.S. House, 90th Congress, PB 179-541, 20 July 1968, Washington, Govt. Printing Office.
Cox, Donald, *American Explorers of Space.* Maplewood, N. J., Hammond, 1967.
Downing, Rev. Barry H., *The Bible and Flying Saucers.* Phila., Lippincott, 1968.
Keyhoe, Donald E., *Flying Saucers: Top Secret.* New York, Putnam, 1960.
Lorenzen, Carol & Jim, *UFOs: The Whole Story.* New York, Signet Books, 1969.
Olsen, Thomas M., *The Reference for Outstanding UFO Reports.* P. O. Box 57, Riderwood, Md., UFO Information Retrieval Center, 1966.
Ruppelt, Edward J. *The Report of U.F.O.s.* Garden City, N. Y., Doubleday, 1956.
Saunders, David R. & Harkins, R. R., *UFOs Yes! Where the Condon Committee Went Wrong,* New York, Signet Books, 1968.
Shklovskii, I. S., & Sagan, Carl, *Intelligent Life in the Universe.* San Francisco, Holden Day, 1966.

Sullivan, Walter, *We Are Not Alone.* New York, McGraw-Hill, 1964.
Vallee, Jacques, *The Anatomy of a Phenomenon.* Chicago, Regnery, 1965.
Vallee, Jacques & Janine, *Challenge to Science: The UFO Enigma.* Chicago, Regnery, 1966.
Weaver, Kenneth F., "Remote Sensing: New Eyes to see the World," *National Geographic,* Jan. 1969, pp. 47-73.
Zigel, Felix, "Unidentified Flying Objects," *Soviet Life,* Feb., 1968.

4. COMPUTERS, FOOD AND PEOPLE

Ehrlich, Paul, *The Population Bomb.* New York, Ballantine Books, 1968.
Graham, Billy, *World Aflame,* New York, Pocket Books, 1965.
Paddock, William & Paul, *Famine-1975.* Boston, Little, Brown, 1967.

5. THE WORLD CHURCH

Latourette, Kenneth S., *Christianity Through the Ages,* New York, Harper & Row, 1965.
Murch, Taylor, Walvoord, & Paton, *The Coming World Church.* Lincoln, Nebr., Back to the Bible Publications, 1963.

6. WORLD WAR III PROSPECTS

Calder, Nigel, *Unless Peace Comes.* New York, Viking Press, 1968.
Chemical and Bacteriological Weapons: The Effects of their Possible Use. New York, United Nations Publications, 1969.
Joint Committee on Atomic Energy—US Congress, *Scope, Magnitude and Implications of the U.S. Antiballistic Missile Program.* Washington, Govt. Printing Office.
Norlie, Peter, & Popper, Robert D., *Social Phenomena in a Post-Nuclear Attack Situation.* Arlington, Va., Champion Press, 1961.
Rathjens, George W., "The Dynamics of the Arms Race," *Scientific American.* Apr. 1969, pp. 15-25.
Sakharov, Andrei D., *Progress, Coexistence & Intellectual Freedom.* New York, Norton, 1968.
Salisbury, Harrison E., *War Between Russia and China.* New York, Norton, 1969.
Stonier, Tom, *Nuclear Disaster.* Cleveland, World Publishing, 1964.

7. THE ANTICHRIST

Dixon, Jeane, & Noorbergen, René, *My Life and Prophecies.* New York, Morrow, 1969.

Levin, Nora, *The Holocaust*. New York, Crowell, 1968.
Montgomery, Ruth, *A Gift of Prophecy: The Phenomenal Jeane Dixon*. New York, Bantam Books, 1965.
Orr, William, *Antichrist, Armageddon and the End of the World*. Temple City, Calif., Grace Gospel Fellowship Publishers, 1966.
Orwell, George, *1984*. New York, New American Library, 1961.
Steiner, Jean F., *Treblinka*. New York, Signet Books, 1968.

8. THE RAPTURE QUESTION

Feinberg, Charles L., *Prophetic Truth Unfolding Today*, Westwood, N. J.: Fleming H. Revell, 1968.
Larkin, Clarence, *Dispensational Truth*. Phila., Rev. C. Larkin Estate Publishers, 1918.
Murray, Andrew, *Abide in Christ*. New York, Grosset & Dunlap, n.d.
Walvoord, John P. *The Rapture Question*. Grand Rapids, Mich., Dunham Publishing, 1957.

9. JESUS THE CHRIST AND HIS KINGDOM

Albright, W. F., *From the Stone Age to Christianity*. Garden City, N. Y., Doubleday, 1957.
Durant, Will, *Caesar and Christ*. New York, Simon & Schuster, 1944.
Engel, Leonard, "A Fifth Ice Age Is Coming," New York *Times* Magazine, Dec. 7, 1958.
Fuller, Buckminster, "Man with a Chronofile," *Saturday Review*, Apr. 1, 1967.
Herberg, Will, *Judaism and Modern Man*. New York, Harper & Row, 1951.
Lapp, Ralph E., *Matter*. New York, Time, Inc., 1963.
Pfeiffer, John, *The Cell*. New York, Time, Inc., 1964.
Rehwinkel, Alfred M., *The Flood in the Light of the Bible, Geology and Archeology*. St. Louis, Concordia Publishing, 1951.
Sanderson, Ivan, "The Riddle of the Quick-Frozen Mammoths," *Saturday Evening Post*, Jan. 16, 1960.
Schneider, Johanne, *Jesus Christ: His Life and Ministry*. Washington, D.C., Christianity Today Publications, 1968.
Stromberg, Gustaf, *The Soul of the Universe*. North Hollywood, Calif., Educational Research Institute, 1948.
Trueblood, David E., *The Humor of Christ*. New York, Harper & Row, 1964.
_____. *Philosophy of Religion*. New York, Harper & Bros., 1957.
Unger, Merrill F., *Unger's Bible Dictionary*. Chicago, Moody Press, 1966.

Walvoord, John P., *The Millennial Kingdom*. Grand Rapids, Mich., Dunham Publishing, 1959.

Wilson, Mitchell, *Energy*. New York, Time, Inc., 1963.

10. A PROBABLE SCENARIO

Brown, Joe D., *Can Christianity Survive?* New York, Time-Life Books, 1968.

Conway, J. S., *The Nazi Persecution of the Churches, 1933-45*. New York, Basic Books, 1968.

Eddlemon, H. Leo, *et al., Last Things*. Grand Rapids, Mich., Zondervan Publishing, 1969.

Feinberg, Charles L. *et al., Focus on Prophecy*. Westwood, N. J., Fleming H. Revell, 1964.

Joint Committee on Atomic Energy, US Congress, *Impact of Chinese Communist Nuclear Weapons Progress on United States National Security*. Washington, Govt. Printing Office, 1967.

Kirban, Salem, *Guide to Survival*. Huntington Valley, Pa., Salem Kirban, 1968.

Kuhlman, Paul & Paton, John I., *Outline Studies of Prophetic Truths*. Lincoln, Nebr., Back to the Bible Publications, 1959.

Lindaman, Edward B., *Space: A New Direction for Mankind*. New York, Harper & Row, 1969.

Lowell, C. Stanley, *Embattled Wall*. Washington, D.C., Americans United, 1966.

Miller, C. J., "Public School Bible Study: Sectarianism in Disguise," *Christianity Today*, Aug. 1, 1969, pp. 3-5.

Parrott, Bob W., *Earth, Moon and Beyond*. Waco, Tex., Word Books, 1969.

Pollack, John, *Billy Graham*. New York, McGraw-Hill, Book Co., 1966.

Rice, John R., *Bible Lessons on the Book of Revelation*. Murfreesboro, Tenn., Sword of the Lord Publishers, n.d.